I DARE YOU

Lee Rogers
Lead Author and General Editor

Kathleen Dondzila
Associate Editor

missional basics

Scripture quotations marked NIV are taken from the Holy Bible, New
International Version®, NIV®. Copyright © 1973, 1978, 1984, 2011 by
Biblica, Inc.™ Used by permission of Zondervan. All rights reserved
worldwide. www.zondervan.com The "NIV" and "New International
Version" are trademarks registered in the United States Patent and Trademark
Office by Biblica, Inc.™

Scripture quotations marked NLT are taken from the *Holy Bible*, New Living
Translation, copyright © 1996, 2004, 2007, 2013 by Tyndale House
Foundation. Used by permission of Tyndale House Publishers, Inc., Carol
Stream, Illinois 60188. All rights reserved.

Scripture quotations marked "The Message" are taken from *THE
MESSAGE*, copyright © 1993, 1994, 1995, 1996, 2000, 2001, 2002 by
Eugene H. Peterson. Used by permission of NavPress. All rights reserved.
Represented by Tyndale House Publishers, Inc.

Scripture quotations marked ESV are from the Holy Bible, English Standard
Version® (ESV®), copyright ©2001 by Crossway, a publishing ministry of
Good News Publishers. Used by permission. All rights reserved.

Scripture quotations marked NASB are taken from the New American
Standard Bible® (NASB), Copyright © 1960, 1962, 1963, 1968, 1971, 1972,
1973, 1975, 1977, 1995 by The Lockman Foundation Used by permission.
www.Lockman.org

Scripture quotations marked HCSB® are taken from the Holman Christian
Standard Bible®, Copyright © 1999, 2000, 2002, 2003, 2009 by Holman Bible
Publishers. Used by permission. HCSB® is a federally registered trademark of
Holman Bible Publishers.

Theme and cover design by Ben Engle. www.benengledesign.com
ben@benengledesigns.com

ISBN: 0692873015
ISBN-13: 978-0692873015

To my wife and son:
Kiki, you dare me to dream bigger;
Judah, you dare me to be better.

I Dare You

Contents

To Every Campus Missionary
Thank you for daring to share Jesus at school and beyond.
Your stories provide the inspiration contained in these pages.

To The Contributing Authors
We have dreamed and cast vision together throughout these past years.
Thank you for your friendship, partnership, time, and energy.
Let us keep striving in one accord, united for a purpose;
to catalyze a movement of students reaching students.

The stories told within these pages are real. The names of some of the participants have been changed for their privacy.

Introduction

This book is going to challenge you. In fact, you may want to stop reading now, because what follows in these chapters could drastically change your current life and friendships. This book was not written to give you an easy way to trick your friends into following Jesus; that's not a real thing. It wasn't written to make you more popular or likeable; neither of those things will lead people to Jesus. This book wasn't written to make you feel better about yourself; there are already too many self-help books on the market. This book was written to challenge you, so if you don't like to be challenged, close this book now. Still reading? Good. Keep going, if you dare.

The Gospel continually challenges us; there is no way around it. Faith, itself, is a dare, and placing faith in Jesus is the ultimate dare. It's not for the faint of heart; it's for those who would risk the courage of heart and strength of mind to defy the world, to dare to think differently from the prevailing attitudes of self-obsession. It's impossible to share the Gospel with our friends, to dare them to place their faith in Jesus, without also challenging them. This book was written for that purpose; to challenge you, and to help you challenge your friends. Reading this book will be easy, if you can stomach it, but doing what it says will be hard. This is a dare to spread the Gospel one challenge at a time. Keep reading. I dare you.

The first part of this book is a dare for you, the reader, to spread the Gospel one challenge at a time. Sharing the transformational power of the Gospel is most effective when we are also transformed by that power. First, you will be challenged to be Gospel-centered, so that the Gospel can affect your entire being. Second, you will be challenged to be Spirit-empowered; to allow the Holy Spirit to work in, through, and with you. Third, you will be challenged to be personally responsible for the mission of God through sacrificial service, uncompromised proclamation, and a commitment to make disciples.

The second part of this book contains 11 challenges that you can use to dare your friends towards faith in Jesus. Help them open the door to faith by challenging them to pray, to serve, or to explore their doubts about God. Dare them to go to church with you, to listen to God, to love like Jesus, or use one of several other dares to help them get in touch with God. To ensure you have fun along the way, each challenge also contains a "fun dare," something you can use to break the ice before moving into more serious territory. Many chapters contain questions to help you have a discussion with your friends, and next steps to continue daring them with faith.

The third part of the book contains the ultimate challenge: "I dare you to place your faith in Jesus." It also contains three tools to help you explain the Gospel, which can be used any time you are daring your friends, as the Spirit leads you. The final chapter is about daring to be different. You will need to be comfortable with being different if you are serious about spreading the Gospel one challenge at a time.

I dare you to keep reading. I dare you to be Gospel-centered, Spirit-empowered, and personally responsible for the mission of God. I dare you to spread the Gospel one challenge at a time.

Lee Rogers
Lead Author and General Editor

Go ahead.
Turn the page.
I dare you.

Part One

A Challenge

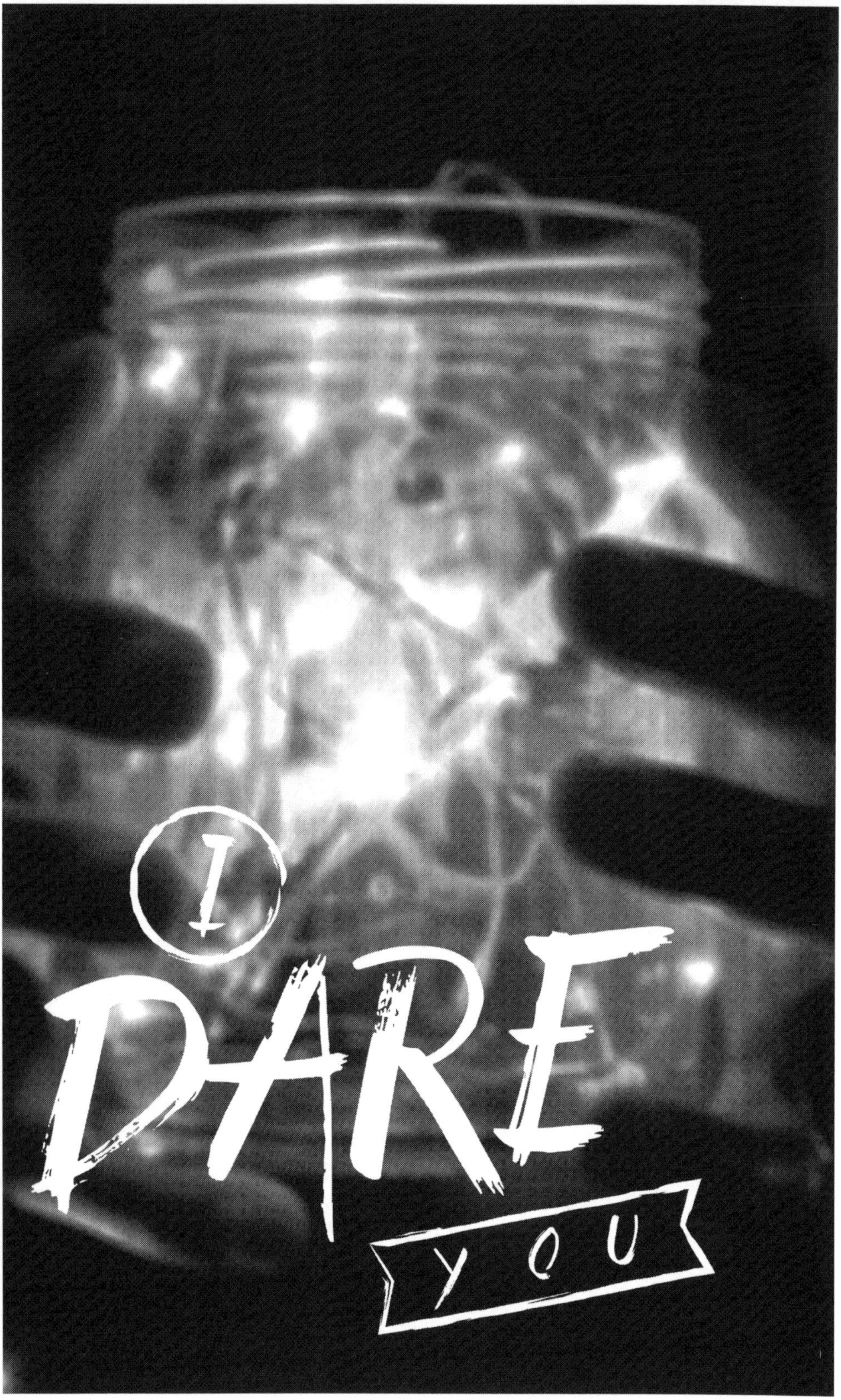
I
DARE
YOU

1
...to spread the Gospel.

"Come on! Do it! You won't." I can still hear the voice of my best friend, Tommy, taunting me from below. I stood nervously looking down at him from 30 feet above.

"How did I get myself into this?!" I kept thinking to myself. We were a couple of bored college students, so one warm September afternoon we gathered a few friends and went looking for fun. Tommy had heard about a swimming hole on the river near school, at the base of a small dam. The water was deep enough to jump into from the top of the old dam, which was—you guessed it—about 30 feet high. Tommy was always searching out this kind of adventure, and because we were buddies, I often ended up going along with him.

I was pretty adventurous myself, but Tommy was more daring than I was. Every once in a while I found myself in an awkward position; I regretted going on the adventure, but I was also faced with the task of following Tommy and completing the challenge. There seemed to be a continuous stream of these situations: launching off the tallest jump on the ski slope at full speed; sprinting under heavy fire to capture the flag at the paintball field; eating the hottest atomic hot wing; trying to get the best reaction and quarter-mile time at the local drag strip in my 1991 Ford Taurus...the list can go on and on. There was no end to our appetite for adventure, or perhaps our stupidity.

I was in one of those awkward, regretful situations on that day. I was standing on top of the dam, and Tommy had just jumped into the river ahead of me. Being the show-off that he was, he had not only leapt from the dam without fear, but he had done a twist in mid-air just to add some style. The girls who had come along with us probably had something to do with this extra bit of showing off. Now, I am not afraid of heights, but I do have some reservations about jumping from those heights. As I approached the edge of the dam and looked down, my reservations got the better of me. The river truly was deep enough to jump into, but if I slipped or jumped in the wrong direction by mistake, I could easily end up falling onto the rocks just a few feet away. I got an uneasy feeling in the pit of my stomach, and I froze.

"Come on!" Tommy taunted. "Do it! You won't." He was working hard at provoking me to jump, but I was still thinking it over. Then he shouted, "JUMP! I DARE YOU!" Time stood still. There he was, standing in the river, directly challenging me to jump. The girls were watching, my heart was pounding, and my mind was racing. I took three steps back, got a running start, and leapt from the top of the dam!

I can't tell you exactly what it looked like as I plummeted through the air towards the water, but I guarantee you there were no twists or flips involved. Instead, it probably resembled a man desperately attempting to run in midair, arms and legs flailing about, a look of shock and terror on his face. It doesn't take long to fall 30 feet; on average it takes just over one second.[1] Yet, in that brief second several thoughts raced through my brain: "I can't believe I just jumped! Am I going to make it? I'm falling! Okay, I think I'm going to hit the water in the right spot. Wait a minute…I'M FLYING!!! This is awesome! I did it!"

Splash! It was over sooner than it began. I plunged deep into the water, swam back to the surface, and headed for the river bank. I emerged from the water attempting to appear self-assured, as though I was entirely confident and had had no reservations at all about jumping, but I'm pretty sure the wild flailing had given me away. I loved flying through the air, but it took a dare from my friend Tommy for me to take the leap. I worked my way back to the top of the dam and jumped a few more times, feeling a little more confident after each attempt. I learned at least two things that day: friends have the power to challenge you to meaningful experiences you might have otherwise missed out on, and a dare can be very persuasive.

The Power of a Challenge

There is something unique about a challenge, and something even more powerful about *being* challenged. A dare is a challenge; to dare others is to challenge them "to perform an action especially as a proof of courage."[2] To accept or attempt a dare is to confront or defy, "to have the courage to contend against, venture, try."[3] Almost everyone grows up facing a dare at one time or another, and researchers have found that male or female, young or old, people are easily motivated to take a dare.[4] We want to be challenged; we desire to be dared.

Accepting a dare is a natural instinct to assert ourselves, to prove that we exist and that we are capable, and it can be a positive experience if it's done in the right way. A dare can be risky, but risk isn't always negative. For example, studies have shown that good leaders are willing to take the right risks, and they often engage in daring behavior.[5] The instinct to take a dare is the same instinct that rises in us when we're told "no, you can't." We naturally want to assert our freedom, defy the limitations, and respond "yes, I can."

My son, Judah, is rapidly approaching his second birthday. He's not even old enough to speak in complete sentences, but he is already asserting himself, working to defy limitations. Recently, I have watched closely as he moves the stuffed animals in his crib, placing them against the railing so he can stand on them. Gaining a slight advantage in height, he holds onto the wooden bars, leans over, and slowly brings one foot all the way up to the top rail, attempting to swing his entire leg over it. He is trying to escape from behind the wooden bars of the crib, working to assert his freedom, to defy the limitations of his baby prison. He works on it everyday, and though he hasn't managed to escape yet, I know he will eventually succeed. Judah is always daring to push the limits of adventure and limitation; jumping off of furniture, trying to stand up on his high chair, climbing high on anything he can scale.

There is also a natural, more subversive challenge that he engages in on a regular basis. It happens when we have to stop him from doing something that could cause him harm, or when he does something disrespectful or disruptive to others. Several weeks ago we were visiting a local small business. Judah walked around the waiting area as I spoke with the owner. He soon decided to explore an electrical outlet, curious about what was in the holes. When he walked up to it and placed his hand on it, I corrected him firmly and loudly by saying, "No."

Surprised, he quickly looked at me to acknowledge my command, but kept his hand on the outlet. Keeping his eyes upon me, he slowly moved his fingers slightly closer to the holes, as though I wouldn't notice. I rapidly moved towards him, more firmly and loudly stating, "STOP NOW."

Knowing that he would be disciplined if he did not stop, he quickly removed his hand from the outlet. I resumed my conversation with the owner, but kept my eyes on Judah, and Judah kept his eyes on me. He was waiting for me to look away so he could try once more. Realizing I wasn't taking my eyes off him, he chose not to touch it. Instead, Judah leaned closer to the outlet and swung his arm towards it, daring to see how close he could get. He kept his eyes on mine, waiting to see what I would do, testing how far he could go. After about 30 seconds, he gave up and turned his attention to something else. Judah knows he can't win every challenge, but he still dares to try. He is not able to express it with his words, but his actions betray an attitude that says, "Don't tell me what I can't do."

Judah is curious, just like his parents, and he constantly seeks new experiences and knowledge by challenging limitations of ability and freedom. My wife and I are willing to take most of the credit for his strong will and curious spirit, but there is also an ancient genetic trait at work, and it goes all the way back to Adam and Eve. They had tremendous freedom and privilege in the garden of Eden, enjoying God's blessing and friendship. The only limitation placed upon them was to not eat the fruit "from the tree of the knowledge of good and evil."[6] Satan, the ancient serpent, came to them and challenged this limitation, manipulating God's instructions and daring them to eat the fruit to gain new knowledge and new experience.

Adam and Eve took this dare, defying the limitations upon them and asserting their freedom. They had been told what would happen if they ate the fruit, but they still dared to do it. All creation has been suffering the consequences since that time. Their actions revealed an attitude that says, "Don't tell me what I can't do." Psychologists call this behavior reactance; it is the motivation to assert freedom or ability when challenged.[7] It is an ancient genetic trait that lies deep inside every one of us. It is a natural human reaction; it is instinctual, and it is powerful.

Satan used the power of the challenge for evil, but God redeems it and uses it for good, daring the world to believe in Him. God's creation issues this challenge, at all times displaying God's "eternal power and divine nature."[8] He also created us with a conscience that reveals what is moral, daring us to recognize the eternal moral source of the Father, Son, and Holy Spirit.[9] God dares us to believe in Him; He engages our tendency for reactance to draw all humanity to Himself. He does not want anyone to perish,[10] and he is even willing to engage our defiant attitudes that express "don't tell me what I can't do" in order to gain our faith.

Jesus understood the persuasive power of challenging people, of daring them to believe in Him. He dared fishermen to leave their nets and become His disciples; He dared the crowds to take up their crosses and follow Him; and He dared a fallen woman brought before Him to leave her life of sin. Through the resurrection, Jesus dared the world to believe that He is God and has conquered the grave. Jesus left the earth approximately 2000 years ago, but He is still daring each person in the world to follow Him, engaging our reactance in order to win our hearts and minds.

Don't Tell Me What I Can't Do

A few years ago I had the opportunity to climb Mount Kilimanjaro, the highest mountain in Africa and the tallest free standing mountain in the world. I've always enjoyed hiking and backpacking, and this challenge was particularly appealing to me. It's not a technically difficult mountain to climb; no special skills are needed, and although it is important to be in good physical condition, you can walk all the way to the top without any climbing equipment. In spite of the ease of the climb, less than half of the people who set out to reach the top are able to finish.[11] That's because no matter how technically easy a climb it is, the altitude can stop even the most physically fit climbers in their tracks.

Altitude can play funny tricks on the body, because the higher you go, the thinner the air becomes. So even though you breathe the same way at a high altitude as you do at a low altitude, your body receives far less oxygen, which can lead to altitude sickness. Mild forms of altitude sickness result in headaches, dizziness, or weakness. The more serious forms lead to fluid on the lungs or brain, and can quickly lead to death if ignored.[12] The only way to fix altitude sickness is to descend to a lower altitude, which is why so many people do not reach the top of Kilimanjaro. Though we had a pretty large group and many of us completed the climb, several had to descend to a lower altitude before getting close to the peak; some got close but couldn't finish; and one person was taken off the mountain on a stretcher.

The peak of Mount Kilimanjaro is 19,340 feet above sea level, which is almost 19,000 feet higher than the altitude I'm accustomed to. I trained hard to prepare myself, ascending a mountain close to our house several times a week in the months leading up to the climb. However, even the top of that mountain was 18,000 feet lower than the peak of Kilimanjaro. Still, I did really well on the climb…until the final day, somewhere around 18,500 feet. I got very sick, very quickly, and began violently throwing up. When I recovered, I ascended another 200 feet, only to fall violently ill once again. By this point I had little or no water left in my body, a headache was coming on strong, I was dizzy, and all I wanted to do was take a nap. I'd never felt as weak and worn out as I did at that moment.

I sat down and considered my situation. I was less than 700 feet from the summit, and for the first time I wasn't sure I could do it. I started to seriously think about giving up; I'd made it pretty far, and no one would blame me for stopping now. I shut my eyes for a few seconds and my body instinctively relaxed; I was falling asleep. My climbing buddy grabbed my shoulder and shook me until my eyes opened. I turned to him and fearfully confessed, "I don't know if I can keep going."

Another member of our party overheard me and said, "Then maybe you shouldn't." Though his words were given in the form of a suggestion, the tone of his voice made his opinion clear; he didn't think I could do it, and he was telling me to give up.

I am quite certain he said it because he was concerned for my well-being, but there was just something about *how* he said it that aggravated and motivated me deep inside. Maybe it was my stubbornness or pride, perhaps I didn't want to disappoint those who had helped me get this far, or maybe it was the human tendency for reactance rising up in me; whatever it was, an instinctual resistance took hold of my mind. I considered his suggestion to be a challenge, a dare to defy his opinion and my own fatigue, to persevere and reach the peak. A shot of adrenaline entered my bloodstream as I defiantly thought to myself, "Don't tell me what I can't do."

I stood and moved upwards toward the peak. Every step required focus I couldn't muster, and energy I didn't possess. My determination was daring my body to keep going. One of the mountain guides walked alongside me, singing songs to encourage me, his voice challenging me onward. I began to stumble to the left and to the right, but he put his arm around my shoulder to steadied my walk, daring me not to give up. Less than one hour from the time I had been ready to give up, I summited Uhuru Peak, the highest point on the tallest freestanding mountain in the world.

I was challenged by the suggestion that I could not do it, and it was that challenge that motivated and energized me to achieve something I wasn't otherwise capable of. It was the dare to keep going that got me to the top, and it ended up being one of the most powerful moments of my life. Although the defiant attitude that declares "don't tell me what I can't do" can get us into trouble, it also has the remarkable ability to push us forward into powerful moments and experiences. What if we could engage that attitude to help our friends find faith in Jesus? What if we dared them to a powerful moment of experiencing the Holy Spirit? What if we, like Jesus, dared the people we know to believe in Him?

Jesus: The Master of the Dare

Jesus is the master of the dare. Early in his ministry, He was walking beside the sea of Galilee when he encountered two fisherman; they were brothers, Simon (later called Peter) and Andrew. They were working, throwing their nets into the lake to catch some fish, when Jesus disrupted their lives with a challenge. He dared them, "Come, follow me, and I will send you out to fish for people."[13] He next dared another set of brothers, James and John, who were also fishing. All four immediately left their nets to follow Jesus. He challenged them with a vision; they would learn to capture the hearts and minds of people. Jesus dared them with purpose, and they accepted his dare with enthusiasm. Challenging others like Jesus did requires *daring with purpose*.

Jesus was praying and meeting privately with His disciples when He challenged them once again. He dared them, "Whoever wants to be my disciple must deny themselves and take up their cross daily and follow me."[14] When people took up a cross it meant they were sentenced to execution, and the cross would be the instrument of their suffering and death. Jesus was daring His disciples to give up their lives to follow Him, to "deny themselves." The word "deny" is the opposite of "confess," to fully confess Christ as Lord means that we also deny ourselves.[15] Jesus dared them with the cross, because it is "the essence of discipleship."[16] Challenging others like Jesus did requires *daring with the cross*.

One day Jesus was teaching in the temple in Jerusalem when some religious leaders brought a woman who was caught in adultery before Him. She must have been humiliated as they announced her sin to Jesus. They were using her, attempting to manipulate Jesus by asking Him if she should be stoned to death as the law commanded, but He refused to debate them. Instead, He challenged the accusers to throw the first stone, but only if they were without sin. It was an impossible dare, and gradually they all walked away. Jesus asked her, "Does no one condemn you?" No one condemned her because no one was without sin. He said, "Then neither do I condemn you," and He dared her, "Go now and leave your life of sin." According to the law she deserved death, but Jesus dared her with grace. Challenging others like Jesus did requires *daring with grace*.

Jesus is the master of the dare. He gained disciples by challenging them with purpose, appealing to their tendency to respond to a meaningful dare. He wasn't afraid of daring them with the most difficult requirement of discipleship, to deny themselves. He challenged His disciples with the cross, and they almost unanimously responded with a lifetime commitment, most of them suffering and dying for the cause of Christ. Jesus knew how to dare with grace, silencing those who would hold us to the law, and providing an escape from condemnation. The list of His dares and challenges could go on and on, but the point is this: Jesus understood the importance of challenging people in order for them to believe. As followers of Christ, we can also learn how to effectively challenge others and provoke them to belief. We will never become as effective as He is at challenging others, for Jesus is the master of the dare, but we must do our best to dare our friends as the Master did.

What do you dare me to do?

Last summer the theme of our youth camp was "I Dare You." It was the perfect theme, fitting so well with the activities of youth camp; I dare you to earn points for your team; I dare you to get in the mud pit; I dare you to run this relay; I dare you to do a belly flop…you get the idea. The real heart behind the theme was the ultimate dare: I dare you to place your faith in Jesus, to trust Him with everything, to surrender your entire being to His will. We had a powerful experience as many students accepted the dare, returning home with new, or renewed, passion for the Gospel.

As is our tradition, we had T-shirts to go along with theme. They were simple T-shirts with the words "I Dare You" on the front in big letters. Two weeks after youth camp, I was in a restaurant with my friend, Doug, and a few others. Doug was wearing his "I Dare You" T-shirt. As we waited in line to order our food, a stranger saw his shirt and approached us, excitedly asking, "What do you dare me to do?"

Doug took a moment to think about it. Seeing that the man was with his wife, Doug replied, "I dare you to stand up on a chair and declare to this entire restaurant that you love your wife."

Sure enough, the man took Doug up on his dare, and stood on the closest chair. He asked for the attention of the entire restaurant and then declared his undying love for his wife. The entire restaurant, at first stunned at the unusual occurrence, soon cheered and applauded the man in response.

Doug shook the man's hand, and as they laughed together, Doug challenged him once more. "Actually, that wasn't the real dare. The real dare is that I dare you to place your faith in Jesus." At first the man didn't quite know what to say, but soon he and Doug were in the middle of a conversation about the Gospel.

Several minutes later, when the conversation was over, Doug said goodbye and rejoined our group. "That's the third time in two weeks that's happened to me. Every time I wear this shirt I end up talking to someone about Jesus, or praying with them. It's the perfect conversation starter."

"Really?!" I said, still amazed at what I'd just witnessed. We were realizing the power of a simple statement on a T-shirt, and we were realizing the power of the dare. Perhaps more importantly, we were realizing the power of the question, "What do you dare me to do?"

The question "what do you dare me to do?" is a positive, curious, and interactive expression on the same wavelength as the defiant "don't tell me what I can't do." Both are rooted in defying limits, expressing freedom, and demonstrating ability; both initiate a challenge. However, when someone *asks* for a dare, it's far more agreeable because it's an invitation to dare. When this man approached Doug he was inviting Doug to dare him, he was asking for something, and in doing so he was opening the door to a conversation. This is important, because most people who place their faith in Jesus do so through a friend who explains the Gospel one-on-one through a conversation.[17] We can effectively dare our friends to put their faith in Jesus through friendship and conversation, and it's even possible to have them ask us for the dare.

Open the Door to Faith

Make no mistake, most people surrender their lives at the foot of the Cross because of "the loving persistence and friendship of someone close to them: a spouse, a friend, a family member."[18] Daring our friends to place their faith in Jesus is a great way to be persistent, and a great way to be a friend. There are two easy approaches to daring our friends; one is to bring it up in a conversation, and the other is to get them to ask us for a dare. Either way, daring your friends will lead to a great conversation, great memories, and great opportunities to talk about Jesus.

One of the keys to sharing Jesus with your friends is to keep bringing Him up, because it takes more than one encounter with the

Gospel before most people are ready to do something about it. In fact, most people must hear the Gospel 7.6 times before they develop faith to believe in Jesus.[19] Advertising experts believe that you must hear about a product about seven times before you will actually purchase it.[20] So they play the same ads over and over and over again. And it works! Now the Gospel is *NOT* a product that we sell or that people buy, but there is a very real sense in which our lives, actions, and speech should promote faith in Jesus. Daring our friends to place their faith in Jesus may be just one of several encounters they need to have in order to believe, so what we are really trying to do is *open the door* to faith in Jesus. They may be ready to walk through that door, or they may need to be dared a few more times. If you can open the door to faith through a dare, you've achieved a powerful step in helping your friends believe.

One simple and easy way to get your friends, or really anybody, to ask "what do you dare me to do?" is to do what Doug did—wear a T-shirt that says "I Dare You" on it. Every time He wears the shirt in public, Doug has an interaction that leads to the Gospel, or prayer, or a new friend. You can get an "I Dare You" T-Shirt at www.initiateconversations.com.

www.initiateconversations.com

Of course, you can always make your own shirt if you choose to do so. When you wear the shirt, be prepared for anyone to ask you "what do you dare me to do;" not just your friends. Think in advance of what you will dare when asked, and about having a conversation around the subject of the dare. Most importantly have fun—because daring someone should be fun. If you decide not to wear an "I Dare You" T-shirt, just keep in mind that you will have to initiate a conversation in order to dare your friends.

One Challenge at a Time

Daring our friends to place their faith in Jesus is the ultimate dare, and it can be life changing. When the Holy Spirit leads you to do it, you should give this dare to your friends. In the meantime, the goal of sharing the Gospel has to center on opening up the door to faith, or helping our friends move through that door, even if it takes several dares and conversations to get there. Since it takes multiple encounters for someone to gain faith to believe in Jesus, we should be prepared to give multiple dares and challenges. This book has been written to help you do just that.

There are a lot of different things you can dare your friends to do that will open the door to faith in Jesus. Sharing the Gospel isn't about one big presentation, or memorizing the latest evangelism technique, or speaking in front of a large crowd. Sharing the Gospel is about our everyday encounters with our friends, family, neighbors, and even strangers. It's about challenging them through our own commitment to Jesus by being Gospel-centered, Spirit-empowered, and personally responsible for the mission of God. If our lives are lived through the filter of the Gospel, with the power of the Holy Spirit, and attuned to God's mission, then there is a sense in which everything we do becomes a dare to our friends to consider Jesus. It's some of those everyday elements of following Jesus that have the potential to become powerful challenges to our friends, opening the door to faith.

Dare your friends to have a conversation with you about the Bible, church, or who they believe Jesus was. Dare them to join your prayer group at school, or simply to pray to God on their own for two weeks and listen for His response. Dare them to read the Bible and discuss it with you. Dare them to serve alongside you, to love sacrificially, or to consider all the things God has blessed them with. Dare them to come to church with you for a month, to see how it could make a difference in their lives. Dare your friends to explore their doubts about God, to ask God's help to change something they don't like, or ask the Holy Spirit to give you a dare specifically for each friend or situation. Every dare in this book can be used at anytime as the Spirit leads you, but they are also designed to be particularly effective during certain seasons, holidays, or months of the year. Each of these dare chapters will indicate the best time to put it to use.

The dares in this book won't just help you open the door to faith in Jesus for your friends, they will also help you to grow in your own faith as you read and participate. You will be dared to be Gospel-centered, Spirit-empowered, and personally responsible for the mission of God. Being Gospel-centered means that all our life is affected by Jesus; everything about us passes through the filter of the Gospel. Being Spirit-empowered means we allow the Holy Spirit to work in, through, and with us. Being personally responsible for the mission of God means we are intentional in sacrificial service, proclaiming the Gospel, and making disciples. All three of these personal challenges are important to spreading the Gospel, because each deeply transforms us, helping us more effectively communicate what it means to live a life of faith.

I Dare You

I dare you to spread the Gospel one challenge at a time. I dare you to pray for your friends, asking God to provide opportunities to challenge them to faith in Jesus. I dare you to get the T-shirt and to wear it all the time in order to start conversations and dare your friends. I dare you to challenge your friends like Jesus challenged His followers: dare with purpose, dare with the cross, and dare with grace. I dare you to be persistent, opening up the doors to faith and helping your friends walk through by challenging them consistently. I dare you to never give up. I dare you to be Gospel-centered. I dare you to be Spirit-empowered. I dare you to be personally responsible for the mission of God.

[1] http://www.greenharbor.com/fffolder/speedtime.pdf

[2] "Dare," in *Merriam-Webster Dictionary*, 2017, https://www.merriam-webster.com/dictionary/dare

[3] Ibid.

[4] Genevieve Boland, "Taking a Dare," *The Pedagogical Seminary* 17, no. 4 (1910): 510-511.

[5] Ibid.

[6] Genesis 2:17 NIV

[7] Lijiang Shen and James Price Dillard, *The SAGE Handbook of Persuasion: Developments in Theory and Practice* (Thousand Oaks, CA: Sage Publications, 2013), 167-179.

[8] Romans 1:20

[9] Romans 2:14-15

[10] 2 Peter 3:9

[11] https://www.climbkilimanjaroguide.com/kilimanjaro-facts/

[12] http://www.altitude.org/altitude_sickness.php

[13] Matthew 4:19 NIV

[14] Luke 9:23 NIV

[15] Walter L. Liefeld and David W. Pao, "Luke," in *Luke–Acts*, vol. 10 of *The Expositor's Bible Commentary Revised Edition*. ed. Tremper Longman III and David E. Garland; Accordance electronic ed. (Grand Rapids: Zondervan, 2007), 175.

[16] Leon Morris, *Luke: An Introduction and Commentary*, vol. 3 of Tyndale New Testament Commentaries. IVP/Accordance electronic ed. (Downers Grove: InterVarsity Press, 1988), 253.

[17] William Fay, *Share Jesus Without Fear* (Nashville: Broadman & Holman Publishers, 1999), 12.

[18] Michael Green, *One to One: How to Share Your Faith With Confidence* (Nashville: Moorings, 1995), 11.

[19] Fay, 11.

[20] Will McRaney Jr., *The Art of Personal Evangelism: Sharing Jesus in a Changing Culture* (Nashville: Broadman & Holman Publishers, 2003), 166

2
...to be Gospel-centered.

"Hi Mr. Rogers, this is Nate. I wanted to talk to you about my school. Could you give me a call?" Nate was a sophomore at an inner-city high school, and he was also a Campus Missionary; a student committed to sharing Jesus at school. He had made his commitment two years before, and he'd been sharing the Gospel with his friends and his school ever since. Although Nate was only in 10th grade, he'd started to think in big terms about what he could do to share Jesus as a junior or senior.

Nate had already started a Christian club in his school as a platform for sharing Jesus. He also had a great group of friends, some of whom he had led to faith, that worked together to encourage and hold one another accountable. The club was regularly conducting outreaches on their campus, finding ways to serve other groups within the school, and holding fun events and activities that were open to the entire student body. They were already having some success, but Nate wanted to do more to share the Gospel, and he wanted to do it in a way that would have the largest impact possible. He wanted to challenge his school, to dare his classmates to be transformed through faith in Jesus.

Nate's school was an inner-city school, with inner-city challenges. The school district was working hard to provide a stable environment in which students could gain an education that would prepare them for life after graduation. Still, the school looked quite different from many high schools in the United States: all students had to wear uniforms; there were security officers around just about every corner; and it wasn't unusual for fights to break out between students on any given day. Like many schools, they were fighting against the infestation of drugs, unstable home situations, and severe financial and moral poverty. The school was doing an excellent job educating students in extraordinarily difficult circumstances, but addressing core character and community issues was beyond the school's ability. Though faculty and administration were doing their best to provide character education, there are some things a public school just cannot transform, no matter how hard it tries.

Nate was motivated with compassion to do something about the deep challenges students faced in his school. He knew that character transformation comes from the Holy Spirit, not school rules or classes. God was not something the school could consider talking about, but Nate could. He began to think and pray about how God could use him and the Christian club to affect spiritual change at school. God gave him a vision to provide a school assembly to communicate a positive and fun character-education message to his fellow students. On the same day, in the evening, his club would hold an event and invite the entire school population. At that event, they would share the gospel and talk about its power to transform individual lives, as well as entire communities.

That's why Nate was calling me. Part of my work with Youth Alive® is to help churches and clubs serve schools by providing resources and tools to meet the needs of the school community. A school assembly is one of those tools, always supplemental to the long-term presence of the Gospel in schools through Campus Missionaries and Christian clubs. So, Nate and I had a conversation; he talked about his commitment to be a Campus Missionary and how he had started a Christian club, and we set an appointment to meet with his principal to discuss his vision for an assembly.

Nate's school was large, nearly 2,400 students, and given the dynamic environment of an inner-city campus, I wasn't sure how the meeting would go. Would the principal know who Nate was? Would he consider Nate's vision worth the time and effort given the deep social challenges the school was facing? I also had some questions about Nate, himself, because to my knowledge we had never met before. What kind of a student was he? What was his reputation? Was he a Campus Missionary in name only, or was he truly being Gospel-centered at school?

All of my questions were answered when Nate and I met with the principal, and as he and I worked together over the coming year to plan the assembly and his Club's evening event. The principal knew exactly who Nate was, not for disciplinary reasons, but because Nate was an outstanding example of character and compassion in the school. Nate shared his idea of an assembly with the principal, and I also explained how the assembly program worked. Nate also shared his vision to have an evening event, held by the Christian club, to share his faith with his classmates. The principal explained that the school could not promote the evening event, but as a student led club, they were welcome to hold an event and advertise it on their own.

As our meeting came to a close, the principal turned to me and said, "Nate is one of the finest examples of character and compassion that we have at this school. I love this vision, and I love that it's coming from a student. I think Nate could make the school assembly his senior graduation project, and I want to personally be his project advisor."

I was amazed; first that the principal knew Nate for his outstanding character, second that he so quickly agreed to the idea, and third that he wanted to be personally involved with Nate's vision. I was impressed. I've seen a lot of bright and committed students who attempt to do the same thing Nate was attempting, but never gain permission, or even get a meeting with the principal. Over the next year, I observed Nate as he worked, prayed, and served in order to fulfill his vision. He was one of the most Gospel-centered students I have ever met, and this was what allowed him to be successful in fulfilling the vision God had given him.

Gospel-Centered

Nate couldn't have gotten as far as he did without a commitment to being Gospel-centered. Everything about his life was affected by the Gospel of Jesus Christ. He wanted to dare his school to believe in Jesus because he was Gospel-centered. He had a reputation for character and compassion because he was Gospel-centered. He understood the transformational power of faith in Jesus because he was Gospel-centered. It was his attitude, speech, and conduct that opened the door for him to share his vision with the principal. It was his commitment to, and involvement in, his church that allowed him to gain the support he needed to make the school assembly and evening event a success. It was his dedication to the Bible that equipped him to share Jesus with his classmates, to live a life consistent with that message, and to personally grow in his commitment to Christ. Being Gospel-centered means our entire lives are filtered, impacted, changed, and transformed by the power of the Gospel.

I think of this every time I make coffee. I love coffee. It's no secret I drink several cups a day, keep a coffee press in my office, and hit up the local coffee drive thru several times a week. However, I'm not as fanatical about having "the perfect brew" as some of my friends are. A lot of things need to go right in order to get a perfect cup of coffee: the right beans, the proper roasting technique, the perfect amount of time between the roast and the grind, a coarse or fine grind, the brewing method, and even more. Since I'm not a coffee snob, any number of those things could go wrong, and I could still enjoy a cup of coffee. However, there is one part of the process that must absolutely work, or the coffee is ruined for me: the filter. If the filter is faulty, or non-existent, then the brew will be partially or entirely non-drinkable. There is nothing worse than taking a sip of coffee, only to realize some of the grounds have made it through the filter and into the cup. It ruins it for me. I don't want any grounds in my coffee. I just want coffee. The filter is key.

Being Gospel-centered is like having our entire lives filtered by and through the Gospel. Everything that goes in, flows out, or takes place in our hearts and minds passes through the filter. Our dreams, hopes, and ambitions pass through the filter. Our attitudes, speech, actions, and relationships pass through the filter. Everything is changed because of Jesus. Being Gospel-centered is not about working to live according to a set of rules, it's about fundamentally allowing the Gospel to shape who we are inside and out so that we are supernaturally shaped by its power.

I'll never forget something Nate said to me as we met together. "We have the cure, the panacea, for all the problems in the world, and it's Jesus." The reason I'll never forget it is because I've never heard a teenager use the word "panacea" before. A panacea is "a remedy for all ills or difficulties,"[1] something to cure all diseases and sicknesses. A panacea is a medical myth, it is fictional, for there is no medical cure for all sicknesses or diseases. However, the Gospel-centered believer knows that the panacea is a spiritual reality; it's not a pill, it's Jesus, and He is the solution for all problems and challenges in life.

There are many things that help us be Gospel-centered, but three major points are evident in Nate's story: he was focused on grace, belonged to the Body, and was immersed in the Word. If you want to dare your friends to place their faith in Jesus, then I dare you to be Gospel-centered.

Focused on Grace

The Gospel is all about grace from God to us. The Apostle Paul wrote in Ephesians 2:8-9, "For it is by grace that you have been saved, through faith—and this is not from yourselves, it is the gift of God—not by works, so that no one can boast."[2] It is only the grace of God, by the sacrifice of Jesus, that saves us. Placing our faith in Jesus Christ is the only thing we can do to receive this grace. This is important, because it doesn't only affect where we place our faith, but it should also affect how we think about it. We can't work for grace. We can't "be good" in order to earn it. If we ever try to dare our friends with the Gospel by telling them to "be good" in order to be saved, then we are not giving them the true Gospel. Faith in Jesus will truly affect our behavior, but it is not our behavior that saves us, it is God's grace, given to us in response to our faith.

Grace should affect our entire mindset, changing how we think about our friends, family members, and communities. Knowing that we cannot save ourselves, but that we are saved by God's love and compassion, must determine our attitude. When I walked around Nate's school with him, I was amazed at how many people knew him, talked with him, and were friends with him. He wasn't what you might describe as a "popular" student; there was nothing cutting edge about his clothes, he was not an all-star athlete, and he never acted out to gain attention. Nate simply made an effort to be friends at all times, to respect every person, to be humble with everyone he met. God's grace shaped Nate's attitude, enabling him to have a good relationship with many people at his school.

It was clear that his principal thought him to be a better student than most, but Nate did not see himself as a better *person* than anyone else. He knew he could not save himself; it was only God's grace that made him who he was. He was motivated to share Jesus, not because he wanted everyone to behave like he did, but because God's grace had the power to transform every person and family connected to his school. Nate knew that he was not the answer to his school's problems—Jesus was. His humble attitude paved the way for him to challenge his school with faith in Christ. His motivation is summed up in the simple children's chorus: "Jesus loves me, this I know, for the Bible tells me so."

It wasn't only Nate's attitude that was impacted by God's grace, his speech was also transformed. Everyone knew he was a follower of Jesus, not because of his good behavior, but because he talked about his faith on a regular basis. It didn't surprise the principal that Nate wanted to have an event at night to share his faith; he knew Nate talked about his faith all the time. It wasn't awkward; it was normal. Jesus, faith, the

Bible, and the church were regular topics of conversation for Nate. The more he talked about his faith, the more comfortable he and everyone around him became with it.

A lot of Christians think it's awkward to talk about their faith. The Gospel is confrontational and it demands a response; it's always awkward for *someone* when the Gospel is shared. However, it doesn't have to be awkward for us. It *shouldn't* be awkward for us. We should already be talking about the Gospel in our everyday conversations; thanking God for our blessings, talking about what happened at church or youth group, or praying with our friends when difficulties come their way. The more we talk about it, the less awkward it becomes. There are any number of ways your faith in Jesus could make its way into your daily conversations.

If we allow the grace of God to change our attitudes and our speech, our friends will not only be used to hearing about our faith, they will expect it. That's what happened for Nate. His entire life was affected by grace; his attitude and his speech were just the starting points. Being Gospel-centered means being focused on grace.

Belonging to the Body

Nate's vision was tremendous, and although it was inspired and guided by the Holy Spirit, I knew he would need help from his church in order to see it become a reality. Nate didn't come from a large church; he didn't have a full-time youth pastor helping him out, and the church he attended had limited resources. This is always a concern, because it usually takes a whole church effort to have a successful outreach on the scale Nate had in mind, and the youth pastor almost always plays a major role. When Nate and I met with the leaders at his church, I quickly found out he was an integral part of the church; he didn't just attend, he belonged. They were willing to get behind his vision no matter what it took.

The church is the body of Christ, and it is something Jesus always intended us to be a part of. Paul wrote in Ephesians 1:22-23, "God placed all things under His (Jesus) feet and appointed Him to be head over everything for the church, which is His body, the fullness of Him who fills everything in every way."³ I am amazed at the percentage of people who identify themselves as Christian, but deny the power and the importance of the church. It's true that the church is not perfect, for although we are Christ's body, we are still in the process of being perfected by His grace. Yet, refusing to participate in the life of the church, denying its importance for a believer, is accepting Jesus' head, but not his Body. That's a really weird image. Scripture also refers to the church as Christ's bride.[4] Imagine saying to Jesus, "I like you, but I can't stand your bride." Ouch!

A church is a gathering of believers, not simply to listen to a sermon or sing worship songs, but to experience the life of faith in Christ as one body, one family, one community. Jesus told his disciples He would begin the church through them,[5] and we are descendants of that promise. The Biblical purpose of the church is to share Jesus with the world, to worship God, to build or disciple a body of believers, and to demonstrate God's love and compassion to the world.[6] The church is to be a Gospel-centered body, and it is a body we must belong to.

The church has taken different forms throughout history and in different parts of the world. In many places the church still meets in houses, or small group gatherings without a church building, which is something the early believers would easily recognize. The disciples could never have imagined the huge churches we have today in some parts of the world, including the United States. However it looks, Jesus made it clear: "For where two or three gather in my name, there I am with them." This is a church, and it can exist almost anywhere. As George Fox, the founder of the Quakers, wrote, "And therefore wherever you are, in prison, or out of prison, where two or three are gathered in His name, there is a church, and Christ the living Head in the midst of them…"[7]

Paul explained some of the special nature of the church in 1 Corinthians 12, writing in verse 12, "Just as a body, though one, has many parts, but all its parts form one body, so it is with Christ."[8] He further explained in verse 27, "Now you are the body of Christ, and each one of you is a part of it."[9] Nate didn't just attend a church, he belonged to a body, and he was a vital part of it. He played an active role in the life of the church, participating in the worship team, the activities, assisting with compassion ministries, and giving help whenever needed. The body valued Nate, and Nate valued the body. They belonged to each other.

Nate needed to raise several thousand dollars to fund his vision. He wanted to bring in the best professional communicators for the assembly, and he wanted to have a festival atmosphere for the evening event; giveaways and prizes, free food, and fun games and activities. He also needed a lot of volunteers to make it happen. His senior pastor let him speak to the whole church and the body of believers got behind him entirely. They all knew and loved Nate, so they wholeheartedly supported him.

The church took offerings and prayed together for the event. The outreach pastor, a volunteer who worked a full-time job outside of church, walked with Nate each step of the way, keeping him focused and helping him think through each challenge. Many from the church volunteered to help, and gave countless hours both in preparation and on the night of the event. The worship pastor coordinated the games and activities, and he'd also been encouraging Nate along the way. Nate was able to challenge his school, to dare them to believe in Jesus, but it wouldn't have been possible if he didn't belong to the body of Christ. A Gospel-centered believer belongs to a Gospel-centered body. Let me be clear, you don't need to be part of a church to receive God's grace, it's our faith alone that is required. However, it's nearly impossible to follow Jesus, the Head, without being a part of the church, His body.

Immersed in the Word

Nate was a Gospel-centered Campus Missionary, not just because he was focused on grace and belonged to the body, but also because he was immersed in the Word of God, the Bible. This is a critical part of being Gospel-centered, and it cannot be overlooked or overstated. You can be focused on grace, and belong to the body, but without immersion in the Bible, being Gospel-centered is impossible. The Bible is verbally inspired by God; it is God's recorded revelation to mankind.[10] The Bible is the guide for our faith, it is never wrong, and it teaches us how to live and respond to life's challenges.[11] As imperfect people, it's possible to err in grace, and for the body of Christ to be imperfect, but God's Word is our guide and correction when things go wrong. It's impossible to be Gospel-centered without knowing the Scriptures.

Nate wasn't just a Campus Missionary, he was also a dedicated Bible Quizzer. Nate spent hours and hours reading and memorizing the Word of God, then competed against other Bible Quizzers several times each year. He didn't do it because of the competition, he did it because he knew it was helping him to be Gospel-centered; it was enriching his inner-being, shaping his mind, showing him how to live. Psalm 119:105 reads, "Your word is a lamp for my feet, a light on my path."[12] The Bible doesn't just give us specific guidance for specific situations, it lights up our entire walk, our entire path, our entire life. If you want to effectively challenge your friends, to dare them to put their faith in Jesus, you've got to allow the light of God's Word to penetrate the darkness of your life, then allow that light to spill into the lives of others.

An early Christian leader and thinker, Ambrose of Milan, said it this way: [Your word is] "a lamp, because it has enlightened the souls of all people and shown the way in the darkness. The way of the lamp is the Gospel; it shines in the darkness, that is, in the world."[13]

It was studying God's Word that helped Nate talk about Jesus all the time. When you read something diligently, whether it's a book, a magazine, or a website, you generally discuss it with others. It's the same with the Bible; if you immerse yourself in the Scriptures, you can't help but talk about them, even with those who don't believe in God. Nate's immersion in the Word was sincere to the point of sacrifice; he gave up the opportunity to participate in the National Fine Arts Festival so he could spend his time focused on memorizing Scripture. This was a big deal, because Nate was an extraordinarily gifted musician and singer, and he would have easily gone far in the Fine Arts Festival. Walking away from the festival to pursue memorizing God's Word also meant he was walking away from scholarship money. I asked Nate about that, and he simply responded, "I'm pretty busy, so I've got to choose one or the other. It's a sacrifice, but memorizing Scripture will help me in the future far more than winning a Fine Arts award or being on a stage." This is what being Gospel-centered looks like, and I long for every new generation of believers to embrace it; to be willing to walk away from things, even good things, that distract us from the best things. Immersion in the Word is non-negotiable if you want to be Gospel-centered.

I Dare You

Nate was given a vision, and he prayed about it and worked on it for over a year. In April 2015, we brought our school assembly to his campus, and Nate fulfilled the requirements of his senior graduation project. When the assembly was over, the principal asked us, "When can you come back? That was the most respectful and attentive our students have ever been for any assembly." That evening Nate's full vision, the vision God had given him, came to pass. More than 800 students and their families came to the high school gym for the Club's evening event. They played games and participated in fun activities, won prizes and giveaways, and ate free pizza. Nate's church, along with a handful of others, paid the bill and provided the volunteers. Nate got up in front of the crowd and did the same thing he was already doing on a regular basis; he talked about God. He challenged his classmates and their families with the Gospel. He dared them to put their faith in Jesus. At the conclusion of the evening, 100 people walked down from the stands in that high school gym and gathered in the center of the floor. They made a decision to place their faith in Christ and begin the journey of discipleship.

I dare you to be Gospel-centered; to allow your entire life to be filtered by the Gospel, to embrace Jesus as the panacea. Nate was a Spirit-empowered Campus Missionary who took on personal responsibility for the mission of God, but it was his Gospel-centered life that gave him the credibility to fulfill the vision God gave him. Nate had credibility with the student body, the principal, his church, and his community. Everyone knew he was a Christian by his speech and his attitude. The members of his church were willing to get behind him in every way, for they belonged to him as much as he belonged to them. His commitment to God's word lit his path, shining the light of the Gospel through his conversations with his friends.

Do you allow everything that flows in and out of your life to be filtered by and through the Gospel? Do you allow the grace of God to fundamentally change your thinking, relying on His grace for your salvation? Or do you try to work for it, thinking that "being good" is earning you grace? Does the grace of God show itself in the things you share with others? Is the Gospel a part of your everyday conversations? Or do you keep it a secret? Do you belong to the body of Christ? Or do you simply attend church? Do you value and embrace church life, and respect the authority of the body? Are you immersed in God's word? Is learning and memorizing Scripture one of your priorities? Do the words of the Bible, the language of the Gospel, find their way into your everyday conversations? If you want to share Jesus, to dare your friends to place their faith in Him, you've got to be Gospel-centered; focused on grace, belonging to the body, and immersed in the Word. I dare you to do it! I dare you to be Gospel-centered!

[1] "Panacea," in *Merriam-Webster Dictionary*, 2017, https://www.merriam-webster.com/dictionary/panacea.

[2] NIV

[3] NIV

[4] Eph. 5:25-27, Rev. 19:7-9

[5] Matthew 16:18

[6] Evangelize the world: Acts 1:8, Matt. 28:19-20, Mark 15:15-16. Worship God: 1 Cor. 12:13. Build/disciple a body of believers: Eph. 4:11-16, 1 Cor. 12:28, 1 Cor. 14:12. Demonstrate God's love and compassion: Psalm 112:9, Gal. 2:10, 6:10, James 1:27. For more on this, see Fundamental Truth #10 at http://www.ag.org/top/beliefs/statement_of_fundamental_truths/sft_full.cfm

[7] George Fox, "Walking in the Power of God: Excerpts from the Letters of George Fox," in *Devotional Classics: Selected Readings for Individuals and Groups*, ed. Richard J. Foster and James Bryan Smith (New York: HarperOne, 2005), 188.

[8] NIV

[9] NIV

[10] 2 Tim. 3:15-17, 1 Thess. 2:13, 2 Peter 1:21

[11] See again 2 Tim. 3:15-17, 1 Thess. 2:13, 2 Peter 1:21, for further reading see http://ag.org/top/Beliefs/Position_Papers/pp_downloads/pp_inspiration_inerrancy_and_authority_of_scripture_08_2015.pdf

[12] NIV

[13] Ambrose of Milan, from "The Prayer of Job and David," 4.4.14, in *Psalms 51-150*. vol. 8 of Ancient Christian Commentary on Scripture. Eds. Craig A. Blaising and Carmen S. Hardin. ICCS/Accordance electronic ed. (Downers Grove: InterVarsity Press, 2007), 331.

3
...to be Spirit-empowered.

"Do you want to come sit with me?" Savannah asked the new girl at school. She had noticed this new student and was making an effort to get to know her and make her feel more comfortable. Savannah is a Campus Missionary—a student committed to sharing Jesus at school. She is always looking for opportunities to demonstrate the love of God by serving her classmates, and building on those opportunities to share the Gospel. So, when a new student showed up at school one day, Savannah knew it would be the perfect chance to live out her commitment as a Campus Missionary.

"Sure," the new girl nervously replied.

"I'm Savannah. What's your name?"

"I'm Jenny."

Jenny stood and walked with Savannah towards Savannah's lunch table. They sat down and Savannah introduced her to the other girls. They talked for the rest of the period and got to know one another better. One of Savannah's friends was wearing a shirt from a Christian school and Jenny asked her about it. The girl explained that she had attended the Christian school when she was younger.

Savannah saw an opportunity and asked, "Jenny, are you a Christian?"

Jenny simply replied, "No," and the conversation moved on to other topics.

Over the next few days Savannah continued to develop her friendship with Jenny. She knew Jenny wasn't a Christian, so she looked for opportunities to talk about her faith in God. Jenny soon revealed she was an atheist; she didn't believe God was real. This didn't affect Savannah's friendship with Jenny, but it did increase her prayers and compassion for Jenny. She began to pray that God would give her the right words to say so she could lead Jenny to Jesus.

Savannah continued to talk about her faith whenever the opportunity presented itself. She talked about her involvement at church, her personal testimony, and she even offered to pray for Jenny when it was appropriate. Eventually, Jenny became irritated with Savannah's faith in Jesus and her attempts to share her faith. It turned out that Jenny wasn't just an atheist, she was, in fact, a militant atheist, and she began to argue against Savannah's faith in God. Through all of this, Savannah continued to be friends with Jenny, working hard to be kind and understanding.

Jenny had gotten her hands on a Bible and brought it with her to school one day. Initially, Savannah thought this was great news, believing Jenny must be getting closer to finding faith in Jesus. However, Jenny had brought the Bible to use against Savannah. She had been marking the Bible up at every point she didn't understand, every verse she felt was contradictory, and every scripture she felt was "dumb" in order to antagonize Savannah and challenge her faith in Jesus; trying to find holes in Savannah's belief and provoke an angry response from her.

Savannah continued to respond to Jenny with kindness. It made her nervous when Jenny questioned her faith, and it bothered her when Jenny attacked the Bible and God's existence, but she tried not to let it show. Instead, she prayed. Jenny's aggravation at Savannah's continued faith in God grew stronger. She went home and began to research how to argue against the Bible and the Christian faith, and she continued to mark her Bible up at every verse she planned to use in her debates with Savannah. One night she even took a picture of her Bible filled with post-it notes, marking the scriptures she questioned. She texted Savannah the picture with the veiled threat, "Have fun trying to defend yourself tomorrow."

Savannah was upset, but she continued to pray for Jenny. She asked the Holy Spirit to give her the right words to say, and to help her stay calm and loving. She also asked the Holy Spirit to speak directly to Jenny. The next day Jenny presented her case against God, and Savannah did the best she could defending her faith. Just as important as the words she said was the attitude she presented—she stayed calm and loving and kind as Jenny argued against her. Savannah's persistence in demonstrating God's love disarmed Jenny and allowed their friendship to continue in spite of Jenny's hostility towards Savannah's faith in God. Jenny continued to test Savannah's faith, but Savannah was ready and determined to help her find her way to Jesus.

Then one day something radically changed—Jenny suddenly told Savannah she now realized God was real and she had decided to become a Christian. God had not only been reaching out to Jenny through Savannah, but also supernaturally. Jenny had experienced unusual dreams—a voice had spoken to her, telling her that she wasn't living in the right way. Jenny was confused at first, but then she realized it was God talking to her. God had spoken directly to her objections against Him, and convicted her of her lifestyle and her choices. Jenny was convinced by her dreams and quickly surrendered her life to Jesus.

Savannah had begun to feel a bit nervous whenever Jenny approached her because she never knew if Jenny was going to argue or debate her. However, when Jenny told her that God had spoken to her in a dream and that she had surrendered her life to Him, Savannah was super excited. She had been faithful in sharing Jesus with Jenny, and the Holy Spirit had finished the work by convincing Jenny of God's existence and her need for His grace. Savannah had done her part, and the Holy Spirit did the rest.

Spirit-Empowerment

Savannah was an ordinary student, who with the help of the Holy Spirit, became an extraordinary Campus Missionary. That's because the Holy Spirit enables us to do things beyond our natural abilities, and even works alongside us accomplish the goal of leading our friends to faith in Christ. Jesus called the Holy Spirit a "Helper," who would be with us and in us.[1] Our empowerment by the Holy Spirit begins when we place our faith in Jesus, because it is the Spirit who washes us clean of sin and gives us a spiritual rebirth.[2] That's what Jenny experienced when she decided to place her faith in Jesus.

Savannah would be the first to tell you that what happened between her and Jenny would not have been possible without the power of the Holy Spirit. That initial movement of the Holy Spirit within us is only the beginning. The Holy Spirit continues to work *in* us, just as Jesus promised, and transforms our character from within—this is the fruit of the Spirit. Not only that, but the Holy Spirit also works *through* us, enabling us to discern what God is saying and to speak to our friends on God's behalf—these are the gifts of the Spirit. The Holy Spirit also works *with* us, alongside us, to lead our friends to Christ—this is the mission of the Spirit.

The Fruit of the Spirit

When Savannah told me how Jenny had challenged her belief in God, even going so far as using the Bible against her, I was curious how she handled it. Has anyone ever challenged something or someone you loved, or attacked one of your core values or beliefs? It's easy to either lose your temper or become impatient in these kinds of situations. Our belief in God is part of who we are as followers of Christ, so in a sense Jenny wasn't just challenging God's existence, she was challenging Savannah's identity as a follower of Jesus.

It feels very personal when someone argues against God's existence, and I've seen a lot of believers get upset and angrily argue for their beliefs. In doing so, they demonstrate their passion for God, but they also demonstrate an ugly side of human behavior that can turn people off to the very message they are trying to present. If we get into an argument, we risk creating an adversary of the person we want to reach. Losing patience, showing frustration, and demonstrating anger are some of the behaviors that can transform *in* us as we allow the Holy Spirit's influence and empowerment to grow in our lives.

The Apostle Paul called the transformation of our character the "fruit of the Spirit." Of course, fruit grows on a plant, a tree, or a vine. However, Paul is referring to a *spiritual* fruit that grows within us, developing our character to be more like that of Jesus. Paul wrote, "the fruit of the Spirit is love, joy, peace, forbearance, kindness, goodness, faithfulness, gentleness and self-control. Against such things there is no law."[3] The fruit of the Spirit grows within us as we allow the Holy Spirit's direction and influence in our lives to expand.[4] As this Spirit-empowerment develops, our character is transformed.

The fruit of the Spirit doesn't necessarily change our emotions, or how it feels when we are challenged or face a frustrating situation. Instead, the fruit of the Spirit empowers us to live out the character of Christ beyond our own ability, so that when challenges and frustrations come our way, we are able to stay calm and focused. I asked Savannah how it felt when Jenny challenged her. She responded, "I was nervous and I was annoyed…but I just tried to stay loving towards her. I tried to do the best I could." Savannah *did* do the best she could, but the Holy Spirit helped her to do even better. Through the fruit of the Spirit, Jenny was able to experience love and grace from Savannah.

The Gifts of the Spirit

Not only does the Holy Spirit work *in* us, but the Holy Spirit can also work *through* us, transforming what flows out of us as we speak to others and interact with them. One of the last things Jesus said to his disciples was, "It is not for you to know the times or dates the Father has set by his own authority. But you will receive power when the Holy Spirit comes on you; and you will be my witnesses in Jerusalem, and in all Judea and Samaria, and to the ends of the earth."[5] In that same gathering, Jesus called the Holy Spirit a "gift" from God the Father, a "promise" that would baptize the disciples in a new and different way.[6] The result of that new baptism—the baptism in the Holy Spirit—was the power to be a witness for Jesus.

It's amazing how each of us has the ability to hear something a little different whenever someone else is speaking, or to misunderstand what was meant by the words that were spoken. That's what happened when Jesus first told the disciples to wait for the gift of the Holy Spirit. They asked Him, "Lord, are you at this time going to restore the Kingdom to Israel?"[7] Israel was occupied and dominated by the Roman Empire, and the disciples seemed to think Jesus was going to lead a revolt against Rome and reestablish Israel as the powerful Kingdom it once was.[8] They misunderstood what Jesus was telling them about the Holy Spirit. It wasn't power to overthrow the government, it was power to be a witness for Christ. That power eventually reshaped history as the disciples went forth and shared the message of the Gospel throughout the known world.

If we aren't careful, we will also misunderstand the purpose behind the power and baptism of the Holy Spirit. It's easy to start thinking that it's all about having an overwhelming experience with God, or that it's only about speaking in tongues. It's true that those are a *result* of the baptism of the Holy Spirit, but Jesus told his disciples the *purpose* of the baptism was an empowerment for His mission throughout the world. If we don't view our empowerment through the Holy Spirit as a supernatural ability to share the Gospel with others, we will misunderstand Jesus just as the disciples did.

There was no mistaking what Jesus meant on the Day of Pentecost, when the disciples experienced the promised baptism of the Holy Spirit. Several thousand people were in that area of Jerusalem when the baptism occurred and the disciples began speaking in tongues. Peter, newly filled with the power of the Holy Spirit, stood up in front of the crowd and preached a powerful message about Jesus, calling the crowd to repent and follow Christ. Acts 2:41 states that about 3,000 people heard the message, responded in faith, and joined the church in Jerusalem on that day.

In the same way that Peter was empowered by the Holy Spirit—with boldness to stand and compelling words to speak—we are also empowered by the Holy Spirit to share the message of Christ with others. You might be surprised to learn that Savannah is actually pretty shy, but through the power of the Holy Spirit, she was able to be a friend to Jenny and have conversations with her about Jesus. This is just the beginning of the gifts the Holy Spirit gives us to help us tell others about Jesus.

In 1 Corinthians 12, the Apostle Paul lists nine spiritual gifts that come from the Holy Spirit. Five of the nine gifts deal directly with speaking: the message of wisdom; the message of knowledge; prophecy; tongues; and interpretation of tongues.[9] The message of wisdom and the message of knowledge happen when the Holy Spirit gives you a piece of information to share with another person; wisdom pertaining to guidance for the future, and knowledge pertaining to information about the past or present. A lot of people believe prophecy means predicting the future, but a prophecy is simply a message from God, spoken by a believer through the power of the Holy Spirit. Have you ever felt like God gave you something to say or to share with someone? That's a prophecy, and it may have been a message of wisdom or knowledge, as well. The Holy Spirit can give you words to say and insight on how to have a conversation with someone.

Some of the other spiritual gifts the Apostle Paul lists in 1 Corinthians 12 are faith, healing, and miraculous powers. The Holy Spirit could empower you with one of these gifts as you pray for a friend who is sick or in need of a miracle. God could heal your friend as you pray together, or miraculously change a desperate situation. All the gifts of the Spirit can empower you to be a witness for Jesus, so step out in faith as the Holy Spirit guides you. The Holy Spirit distributes these gifts as he determines,[10] so be sensitive to the Spirit and act in boldness when you sense the time is right.

The Mission of the Spirit

An amazing and supernatural thing happened as Savannah continued to talk with Jenny about Jesus. Although Jenny was combative towards Savannah's faith, the Holy Spirit was working on Jenny's heart and mind in ways that could not be seen with human eyes. Then over a series of nights God spoke to Jenny in dreams, something that only the Holy Spirit could do. That's what eventually pulled Jenny over the threshold of belief in Jesus. Her conversations with Savannah opened the door to faith, and the Holy Spirit firmly convinced her of her sin and of the reality of Jesus.

It's true that the Holy Spirit empowers us in our personal responsibility for the mission of God, but that's not all the Holy Spirit does. In fact, the Holy Spirit has its own mission in the world and is actively working to draw people to Christ, including those that we are also attempting to lead to Him. The Holy Spirit not only works *in* us and *through* us, but also *with* us—alongside us—to lead our friends to Christ. Savannah and Jenny's story is a perfect example of two elements of the Spirit's mission: the Spirit gives witness to Christ; and convicts us of sin, righteousness, and judgment.

Savannah wasn't the only person talking to Jenny about Jesus, the Holy Spirit was also talking to Jenny. In fact, the Holy Spirit is already having a conversation with all the people of the earth, trying to convince them to believe in God, but most people don't recognize that the conversation is happening. Jesus said the Holy Spirit, when sent to the earth by the Father, "will testify" about Him (John 15:26). In other words, the Holy Spirit is the original evangelist—declaring Christ and the Gospel, daring every person in the world to put his or her faith in Jesus. This means even the most combative person, or the person you believe is the farthest from Jesus, is already being spoken to about God by the Holy Spirit. That's why Rebecca Pippert states, "We must never assume that a person will not be open to Christianity."[11] The Holy Spirit is continually conducting a case for Christ throughout the whole world, speaking to every person about Jesus, daring all humanity to believe.[12]

Through the dreams God gave her, Jenny was convicted to change her belief and place her faith in Jesus. This is the impossible task the Holy Spirit does, something we are not capable of doing ourselves: the Holy Spirit convicts people of the error of their ways, of God's righteousness, and about the judgment that is to come. Jesus laid this out plainly for us in John 16 when He was speaking with the disciples about His departure from the earth and the coming of the Holy Spirit. He said, "When He (the Holy Spirit) comes, He will convict the world of its sin, and of God's righteousness, and of the coming judgment."[13]

The word "convict" in this passage means that someone has done wrong, and that there is proof of wrongdoing.[14] It is a conviction associated with crime, fault, error, or sin and suggests the shame of the person who was convicted.[15] To convict someone means they are *convinced* beyond all doubt that what they were doing was wrong. That's really hard to do! Most people don't want to hear about it when they've done something wrong, and they definitely don't want anyone to convince them their entire life is off-course—that's downright offensive to most people. I believe that's the reason God made it the Holy Spirit's job; it's just too difficult for us to do.

Savannah didn't waste time trying to tell Jenny about the evils of her sin, instead she focused on talking about Jesus. That's our job—to talk about Jesus. When you dare someone to put their faith in Jesus, focus *on* Jesus, and let the Holy Spirit do the hard work; convicting that person of sin, righteousness, and judgment.

I Dare You

I dare you to be Spirit-empowered; to allow the Holy Spirit to work *in, through,* and *with* you as you challenge your friends to open the door to faith in Jesus. Savannah is a Gospel-centered Campus Missionary who has taken on personal responsibility for the mission of God in her world, but without Spirit-empowerment, Jenny would likely still be an atheist. That's because without the empowerment of the Holy Spirit, Savannah is limited to her natural abilities. Yet through the fruit of the Spirit and the gifts of the Spirit, Savannah was able to share Jesus with Jenny in effective and friendship-promoting ways. Savannah did her part in God's mission, and as a result, Jenny was ready to respond with faith in Jesus when the Holy Spirit spoke directly to her in her dreams.

Are you allowing the Holy Spirit to work in you and through you? Are you allowing the Holy Spirit to work with you, alongside you? Is the fruit of the Spirit evident in your life, your daily conversations and friendships? Are you desiring and praying for spiritual gifts? Are you open to the Holy Spirit speaking through you? Do you allow the Holy Spirit to convict your friends? Or do you put yourself in the Holy Spirit's place by pointing out their sin? If you want to share Jesus, to dare your friends to place their faith in Him, you've got to allow the Holy Spirit to work *in, through,* and *with* you. I dare you to do it. I dare you to be Spirit-empowered.

[1] John 14:16-17

[2] Titus 3:5

[3] Galatians 5:22-23 NIV

[4] "The Acts of the Sinful Nature and the Fruit of the Spirit," *Fire Bible: Global Study Edition*, Accordance electronic ed. (Springfield, MO: Life Publishers International, 2009), Galatians 5:22-23.

[5] Acts 1:7-8 NIV

[6] Acts 1:4-5

[7] Acts 1:6 NIV

[8] Clinton E. Arnold, "Acts," in *John, Acts*, vol. 2 of *Zondervan Illustrated Bible Backgrounds Commentary: New Testament*. ed. Clinton E. Arnold; Accordance electronic ed. (Grand Rapids: Zondervan, 2002), 225.

[9] A great book on 1 Corinthians 12 and the gifts of the Spirit is Harold Horton's *The Gifts of the Spirit* (Springfield, MO: Gospel Publishing House, 1975).

[10] 1 Corinthians 12:11

[11] Pippert, 115.

[12] Leon Morris, *The Gospel of John*, New International Commentary on the New Testament. Accordance electronic ed. (Grand Rapids: Eerdmans, 1995), 607

[13] John 16:8 NLT

[14] Greek-English Lexicon of the New Testament Based on Semantic Domains, "ἐλέγχω ἔλεγξις ἐλεγμός," Accordance electronic ed., 436.

[15] Thayer's Greek-English Lexicon of the New Testament, "ἐλέγχω," Accordance electronic ed.

I

DARE

YOU

<u>4</u>
...to be personally responsible for the mission of God.

"I can't believe that just happened," Alexa thought to herself as she walked out of the principal's office. She'd been full of optimism and vision when she'd entered the office, but now she was confused and frustrated. She kept going over it in her head. "God, I don't understand. I thought this was something you were calling me to do. Was I wrong? What am I supposed to do now? How can I achieve the vision you've given me?"

Alexa was a Campus Missionary—a student committed to sharing Jesus—at a public charter school in the northeast United States. Towards the end of her eighth grade year, God gave her a vision to start a Christian Club in her school as a platform for serving her classmates and proclaiming the Gospel. She'd prayed about, prepared and organized her vision, and set up a meeting with her principal to discuss how she could proceed. She'd walked into her principal's office well prepared for any questions the principal would ask. However, it was a short meeting, and the principal didn't ask *any* questions; instead quickly responded: "Oh, you can't start a Christian club here. We've already decided we're not going to allow a Christian club."

Alexa sat stunned; she was not expecting this response. When she regained her composure, she asked why. The principal explained that it was too controversial; it was something the school wanted to avoid. Alexa knew the school had many other clubs, and she also knew it was illegal for a public school to discriminate against Christian students if they wanted to form a Christian club. She asked about this, but her principal quickly pointed out that this was a charter school, not a traditional public school. Students choose to attend a charter school, they aren't required to, so the principal said the laws applied to their school a little differently, and she was standing her ground; there would be no Christian club.

Alexa walked down the hallway, all her optimism and hope gone. The vision God had given her wasn't going to happen. Had she misunderstood what God was telling her? She still had a burden for her school, and she still felt a personal responsibility to share Jesus with her friends. Alexa knew the mission of God is to seek and to save the lost—those who haven't yet placed their faith in Jesus—and she believed having a Christian club would be part of her involvement in that mission. How could she make sense of this situation?

"Hi Alexa! See you at lunch?" a girl asked as she walked past. It was Marley, one of Alexa's friends.

Still stunned from the meeting, Alexa took a moment to respond. "Yes…I'll be there." As the words left her mouth, she was struck with compassion. Marley wasn't just a friend, she was one of the classmates Alexa wanted to lead to Jesus. In that moment, Alexa realized that sharing Jesus with her school would look a little different from what she had envisioned. She knew she had to take personal responsibility for the mission of God in her school and among her friends.

Personally Responsible

After Alexa's request to start a Christian club was rejected, there was a moment (maybe a few moments) when she blamed the school for stopping her from sharing the Gospel. However, she also realized—school permission or not—she still had an obligation to share Jesus with her friends. If the Gospel couldn't be shared with her friends through a Christian club, Alexa needed to figure out another way to talk about Jesus with them. She would not be distracted or deterred by this setback; she was taking personal responsibility for the mission of God.

The Apostle Paul was one of the first to be personally responsible for sharing the message of Jesus Christ. He wrote the following:

> All this is from God, who reconciled us to himself through Christ and gave us the ministry of reconciliation: that God was reconciling the world to himself in Christ, not counting people's sins against them. And he has committed to us the message of reconciliation. We are therefore Christ's ambassadors, as though God were making his appeal through us.[1]

First, Paul recounts what God has done; through Jesus He has made things right between God and man. Paul uses the word "reconciliation," which means removing or erasing hostility between two people, groups, or nations.[2] The hostility between us and God was sin, and Jesus erased that sin and put His own righteousness upon us.

Second, Paul explains the responsibility of all believers for the mission of God; we were reconciled by God (vs 18 - the *ministry* of reconciliation), and now we are commissioned to proclaim the good news to others (vs 19 - the *message* of reconciliation). Paul calls us "Christ's ambassadors," an unmistakable title and assignment. More to his point, Paul used the verb form of "ambassador,"[3] meaning we aren't just to *be* ambassadors, we are to *do* the work of an ambassador. An ambassador represented the king or ruler in action, in speech, often to establish or strengthen relationships, and often held one of the highest ranks in the kingdom or nation.[4] To be an ambassador for Christ means we are an important part of God's mission, we establish or strengthen connections to Jesus in our friendships, our actions represent Christ's character and intentions, our mouth speaks the message of Jesus.

Alexa set a great example of what this looks like today. She moved forward from defeat and took personal responsibility for the mission of God through sacrificial service, uncompromised proclamation, powerful teamwork, and a commitment to make disciples.

Sacrificial Service

Alexa decided to use her own resources to serve her friends and to create opportunities to talk about Jesus. She began inviting her friends over to her house for special occasions, often preparing food, games, and entertainment. While many in her school were facing pressure to engage in destructive behaviors at parties, Alexa served her friends by providing "no-pressure parties" where they could relax, hangout, and just have fun together. She threw Christmas parties, Valentine's Day parties, end-of-the-school-year parties, and she even used her birthday party as an opportunity to serve her friends and share the Gospel.

Of course, all of this was also fun for Alexa, but it was also costly. The food had to be purchased, the games and entertainment took time and money to plan, and Alexa had to give up some personal space by inviting her friends into her home. It wasn't just costly for Alexa, her parents and siblings also paid a price in time, energy, money, and space. They, too, believed the cost was worth the sacrifice in order to serve her friends and have an opportunity to share their faith.

Alexa is no stranger to sacrifice; her youth group is heavily involved in *Speed the Light,* an opportunity to "give so others can speed the light of the Gospel to a world in darkness."[5] *Speed the Light* provides equipment for missionaries all around the world through students who give sacrificially. Alexa has been sacrificially giving through *Speed the Light* for years, and her giving is part of her personal responsibility for the mission of God. She sacrifices her own financial resources so the Gospel can be shared across the globe. So, when Alexa came up with the idea to serve her friends by inviting them over to "no-pressure parties," she didn't flinch at the sacrifice it would require.

Jesus told his disciples that He "did not come to be served, but to serve, and to give His life as a ransom for many."[6] Jesus served all mankind by sacrificing His life on the cross for our sins; it cost Him *everything.* If we are going to share Jesus and represent Him accurately, we should also be serving our friends in a sacrificial way. It probably won't cost us *everything,* but it should cost us *something meaningful.* Taking personal responsibility for the mission of God requires sacrificial service to others. Alexa was willing to pay a price to share Jesus with her friends, to sacrificially serve them in order to represent Jesus and gain an opportunity to share the Gospel.

Uncompromised Proclamation

Like a lot of Christian students her age, Alexa has friends at school and friends at church. When she began hosting the parties, she intentionally invited her friends from church to join in; she wanted to bring the two sets of friends together. Alexa and her Christian friends didn't hide their commitment to Jesus or their involvement at church; they openly talked about youth group activities and services. That wasn't the only opportunity to talk about faith. Alexa is a Gospel-centered student, so it was inevitable that her faith came into the conversation from time-to-time. It often happened simply because they prayed over the food before eating.

After the second year of serving her friends by having them over at her house, one of Alexa's friends, Jessica, started coming to church. Alexa was happy about it, but she also felt like something was missing. It was as though she was always close to sharing the Gospel with her friends, but she hadn't quite reached the goal of communicating the hope she had in Jesus. She had been hoping her faith in Jesus would rub off on her friends as she served them and demonstrated the love of Christ, but it hadn't. She was well-liked, all of her friends thought she was nice, they looked forward to the parties, but they didn't seem any closer to putting their faith in Jesus.

Alexa made a common mistake that many Christians make today; she was serving her friends and demonstrating God's love well, but she wasn't intentionally sharing the Gospel, speaking the name of Jesus, or inviting her friends to participate in the life of the church. It's become popular in the last few decades to be very passive about sharing the Gospel. A misguided, but popular viewpoint is that we should be good people, love our neighbors, and wait for them to ask about our faith rather than share it openly. There are three problems with this. First, it doesn't work; our neighbors and friends are willing to accept that we are nice people without asking why. The second problem is more deceptive and more dangerous; when we sacrificially serve our friends, but do not intentionally share the reason why (the Gospel), we have only won them to ourselves and not to Jesus. We are not the message—*Jesus is the message*, and the message is only communicated when we speak His name.

That leads to the third problem—it's unbiblical to think we can communicate the Gospel without intentionally talking about it. The Apostle Paul makes it clear in Romans 10 that we must speak with our mouths in order share the Gospel:

> For everyone who calls on the name of the LORD will be saved. But how can they call on him to save them unless they believe in him? And how can they believe in him if they have never heard about him? And how can they hear about him unless someone tells them?[7]

How will any of our friends ever hear about Jesus unless we *tell* them? Our sacrificial service opens the door for us to share the Gospel, but it can never replace the *necessity* of sharing the Gospel. Being personally responsible for the mission of God means that we open our mouths and speak the name of Jesus, share the Gospel, and proclaim the message of reconciliation.

As Alexa thought about all that had happened and how far she'd come, she began to realize she needed to be more purposeful in sharing Jesus by asking her friends to come to church and youth group events. She reflected, "It's been good, but I've also just been allowing things to happen instead of intentionally sharing the Gospel." Alexa decided to be uncompromising in proclaiming the Gospel, to purposefully speak the name of Jesus, and that's when things really started happening. It wasn't long before two friends, Grace and Marley, placed their faith in Jesus, and that was just the beginning.

Powerful Teamwork

Alexa hadn't forgotten about the vision God had given her in eighth grade to start a Christian club in her school. She met with the principal a few more times over the years, but the principal continued to deny her request. When Alexa made the decision to be more intentional in sharing the Gospel, she started talking about her vision for the club around school. That's when Glenndale, another believer at her school, told Alexa that he had the same vision. They discussed the frustrations Alexa had experienced, and Glenndale decided to try meeting with the principal one more time.

Although Alexa had previously discussed her rights to start a club with the principal, she had always been dismissed. Glenndale decided to take things a step further. When he met with the principal he brought along a copy of *The Equal Access Act*, a law passed in 1984 that protects students from discrimination on the basis of religion, politics, or philosophical belief.[8] Essentially, if a school has any clubs or groups meeting on the campus that are not related to the school curriculum, the school must allow a religious or political group to meet.

Glenndale studied the law and provided a copy for the principal, who quickly changed her decision. Something happened when Alexa and Glenndale joined together to accomplish the same vision. Maybe the principal felt the pressure of having more than one student advocating for the club, or perhaps seeing a copy of the law convinced her she couldn't deny it any longer, or possibly, she'd been ignorant of the law entirely until Glenndale provided her with a copy. Regardless, the vision God had given Alexa years before was finally going to become a reality.

Something supernatural happens when Christians join together to accomplish the goals and visions God has given them. Teamwork makes things happen much more quickly than working alone. Ecclesiastes 4:9-10 explains it this way:

> Two are better than one,
> because they have a good return for their labor:
> If either of them falls down,
> one can help the other up.
> But pity anyone who falls
> and has no one to help them up.[9]

Not only does teamwork generate better and faster results, it also helps us keep one another encouraged when things get difficult. Meeting Glenndale and discovering that God had given him an identical vision breathed new life into Alexa's goal of starting a Christian Club.

Marley, one of the Alexa's friends who put her faith in Jesus, also joined and helped get the club started. They named the club "Unashamed," and 13 students attended the first meeting. They kept inviting more of their classmates, and about 30 attended the second meeting.

Alexa excitedly reported, "We're gonna need a bigger room! I have a friend who is Muslim who came and she has been inviting other people to the club. I am amazed at this opportunity that God has given me."

The next club meeting was even bigger. Alexa wrote, "We had 43 students today and the classroom were are meeting in is too small. We are looking to move into a staff meeting room that has 60 seats to accommodate all the students we have coming. I'm so excited about everything that is happening!"

Being personally responsible for the mission of God means working together with other believers to make a difference whenever possible. It is a powerful way to serve others and to proclaim the Gospel. When more than one person is telling the same story, the story becomes credible. When several people are telling the same story, it becomes factually believable. When several Christians proclaim the same message of the Gospel in a school or community, it becomes so much easier for people to believe and place their faith in Jesus.

Making Disciples

Alexa has been personally responsible for the mission of God through sacrificial service, uncompromised proclamation, powerful teamwork, and she has also begun to disciple her friends who have become Christians. Marley was one of the first of Alexa's friends to follow Jesus, and now she plays a powerful role in building and running the Unashamed Club. Alexa has been intentional in helping Marley understand and grow in her faith, and she has helped Marley develop her own personal responsibility for the mission of God. She made Marley feel welcomed and comfortable at church, made certain she had a Bible, and had regular conversations to see how she was growing.

Marley is a volleyball player, and she decided to invite her entire team to attend the club. She was hopeful and optimistic, but the response of her teammates left her stunned. They almost immediately began making fun of her for being a part of a Christian club. When Marley saw Alexa she explained what happened. Alexa knew what it was like to have a vision crushed, and she encouraged Marley to keep up the good work. She explained that following Jesus is often socially challenging, but that it would help her to become more like Jesus. Alexa told her it was important to keep trying and never give up, and to do her best to continue serving and inviting her friends to know Jesus.

Marley took Alexa's encouragement to heart, and kept on inviting her volleyball team. At the next Unashamed meeting Marley approached Alexa and whispered excitedly, "Alexa! They are all here! All of my teammates are here!" They were thrilled and amazed. God was working through Alexa to disciple Marley, and working through Marley to reach the volleyball team.

One of the last things Jesus said to His followers is recorded in Matthew 28:18-20:

> All authority in heaven and on earth has been given to me. Therefore go and make disciples of all nations, baptizing them in the name of the Father and of the Son and of the Holy Spirit, and teaching them to obey everything I have commanded you. And surely I am with you always, to the very end of the age.[10]

This is known as "The Great Commission," and it centers on two words—make disciples. Being personally responsible for the mission of God means we aren't just inviting our friends to place their *faith* in Jesus, we are also helping them become fully committed *disciples* of Jesus.

The Apostle Paul was also focused on making disciples. He wrote to the believers at Corinth, "Follow my example, as I follow the example of Christ."[11] That is often what making disciples looks like; we are following Jesus, and those we are discipling are following our example. It's not only about what we *do*, it's also about what we verbally teach and share. In his letter to the Philippians, Paul stated it this way: "Put into practice what you learned from me, what you heard and saw and realized. Do that, and God, who makes everything work together, will work you into his most excellent harmonies."[12] Marley is a believer thanks to Alexa's commitment to share Jesus, and now Marley is doing the things she saw Alexa do; in the same way Alexa taught and encouraged her, she is being discipled.

I Dare You

I dare you to be personally responsible for the mission of God; to serve sacrificially, to proclaim the Gospel without compromise, to work together with other believers, and to make disciples as you challenge your friends to open the door to faith in Jesus. Alexa is a Gospel-centered and Spirit-empowered Campus Missionary, but it wasn't until she took personal responsibility for the mission of God that her friends began to hear the message and respond. Through her sacrificial service and uncompromised proclamation, several of her friends placed their faith in Jesus. As a result of her commitment to make disciples, Marley has been transformed and is growing as a follower of Christ. When Alexa, Glenndale, and Marley worked together as a team, Alexa's vision for a Christian club not only became a reality, but grew into a powerful force for the Gospel at her school.

Have you taken personal responsibility for the mission of God in your school, neighborhood, family, or community? Are you serving others sacrificially? Are you proclaiming the Gospel without compromise? Do you speak the name of Jesus and invite your friends into the life of the church? Do you work together with other believers to accomplish God's mission? Or do you only work alone? Are you making disciples? Do you help your friends become fully devoted followers of Christ? If you want to share Jesus, to dare your friends to place their faith in Him, you've got to sacrificially serve, proclaim without compromise, work as a team, and make disciples. I dare you to do it. I dare you to be personally responsible for the mission of God

---

[1] 2 Corinthians 5:18-20 NIV

[2] Moyer Hubbard, "2 Corinthians," in *Romans to Philemon*, vol. 3 of *Zondervan Illustrated Bible Backgrounds Commentary: New Testament*. ed. Clinton E. Arnold; Accordance electronic ed. (Grand Rapids: Zondervan, 2002), 224.

[3] Ceslas Spicq, "πρεσβεία, πρεσβεύω," in *Theological Lexicon of the New Testament*. trans. and ed. James D Ernest. Accordance electronic ed. (Peabody, MA: Hendrickson, 1996) 3:172-176.

[4] Ibid.

[5] http://stl.ag.org

[6] Matthew 20:28 NIV. See also Mark 10:45.

[7] Romans 10:13-14 NLT

[8] View and download the *Equal Access Act:*
http://youthalive.ag.org/campusclubs/downloads/The%20Equal%20Access%20Act.pdf

[9] NIV

[10] NIV

[11] 1 Corinthians 11:1 NIV

[12] Philippians 4:9 The Message

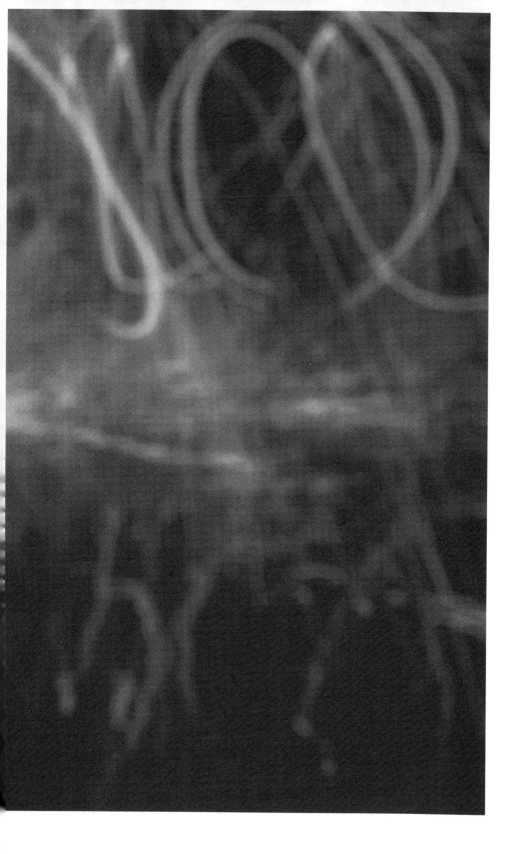

Part Two

I
DARE
YOU

5
...to have a conversation with me.

"Can I ask you a question?" my neighbor asked me.

"Of course. Ask me anything," I replied. My neighbor and I have regular conversations. In fact, I make it a point to start a conversation with her as often as I can. She's not a follower of Jesus, but I am praying for her to become one. I also know that most people who make a meaningful, lasting commitment to Jesus do so through a friend who explains the Gospel in a conversational way.[1] That being the case, I try to have as many conversations with my neighbors as I can. It's only a matter of time until we talk about something connected with the Gospel, church, or the Scriptures. These things are important to me—they are major parts of my life—so it's natural that our regular conversations would touch on these subjects from time to time.

"You might think I'm crazy," she said in a hushed and nervous tone, "but do you think animals go to heaven?" That may seem like an unusual question to you, but it didn't surprise me at all because I know my neighbor is an animal lover. We've had many conversations about animals before. She fosters abandoned animals in need of new homes, volunteers her time at veterinary clinics and rescues, and fundraises for organizations that help animals. I had been feeling for some time that her love for God's creatures would somehow be the bridge connecting her to the Creator. Her question was a great starting point.

But now I was in a dilemma...do animals go to heaven? I answered as honestly as I could. "I don't know. Some people say no, some people say yes. But the Bible has a lot to say about animals, and God cares about how animals are treated." We kept talking for another 30-40 minutes. We spoke about God's concern for the ethical treatment of animals[2], that God provides animals with what they need and has created them to thrive in their various environments[3], and how God was concerned enough to preserve all the animal species in the ark at the time of the great flood. Most importantly, I was able to share how I saw God working through her because of her compassionate action towards animals. God cares about animals, and so does my neighbor. It was the best spiritual conversation we'd had up to that point.

My neighbor didn't make a commitment to Christ that day, but we made massive strides towards the Cross, and we were both changed by the conversation. I got to know her better as she opened up her heart—she was curious about God and Heaven. Her spiritual curiosity led from one revelation to another, leading to reflection and pondering over what it all meant. The conversation opened the door for God to move in her life.

Having conversations is the best way to share the Gospel with others. In this chapter you will be challenged to take one of the most fundamental dares you'll need to effectively share Christ with others: having a conversation. When they ask, "What do you dare me to do?" you reply, "I dare you to have a conversation with me…"

Gospel-Centered

Jesus often engaged others in conversation, and when He did He usually found a way to impart grace or proclaim the Kingdom of God. Consider His conversation with the Samaritan woman at the well in John 4. Jesus dared her to have a conversation by asking a simple question, "Will you give me a drink?" As the conversation continued they spoke together about living water, eternal life, and He revealed Himself as the Messiah. His conversation was centered on the Gospel He'd come to proclaim. The Apostle Paul wrote, "Let your conversation be always full of grace, seasoned with salt, so that you may know how to answer everyone."[4] Not only did the woman come to believe in Christ as a result of this Gospel-centered conversation, but many residing in her town believed also.

Spirit-Empowered

So much of how the Holy Spirit interacts with us involves speaking to other people, so having a conversation is a great opportunity to experience the empowerment of the Holy Spirit. The Holy Spirit can help us take the initiative in conversation because the Holy Spirit works through our voice and speaks to our mind by giving us words to say, even if we think we've got nothing to say.[5] When my neighbor asked me if animals go to heaven, I didn't have a clue how to answer her. But 40 minutes later we were still talking about God, the Scriptures, and animals, thanks to the Holy Spirit. Conversation also creates an opportunity for the person you're having a conversation with to experience the power of the Holy Spirit. In fact, according to Jesus, the Holy Spirit is already in conversation with him or her. The Spirit testifies about Jesus throughout the world, and convicts the world of sin, righteousness, and judgment.[6] The Holy Spirit is continually conducting a case for Christ throughout the whole world, speaking to every person about Jesus.[7]

Personally Responsible for the Mission of God

My neighbor and I didn't start our conversation that day with the intention of talking about God. I simply asked her how she was doing, what was new, and other bits of "small talk." I dared her to have a conversation with me simply by asking her about her life. I believe it's my personal responsibility to start conversations with her, because I know conversation is the most effective pathway for leading someone to the Cross. Even Billy Graham, whose legacy in ministry is speaking to large crowds about Jesus, has stated that mass evangelism is not as effective as when two people have a conversation and one shares about Jesus.[8] Every time I start a conversation with my neighbor, allowing the Holy Spirit to guide me, I'm taking personal responsibility for the mission of God.

Have Some Fun

It's often helpful to have a little fun before you get to the serious dare. This is especially true if you're approached by someone you don't know while wearing your "I Dare You" t-shirt. Break the ice and have some fun by daring them to do something a little kooky. You can always come up with your own dares to break the ice, but a great dare to set up having a conversation with *you* is daring the other person to have a conversation with a *stranger* about an odd topic. For example, when they ask, "What do you dare me to do?" you can respond by saying, "I dare you to go up to a stranger and start a conversation about bananas." You can even point out the person you want them to talk with. Have fun with it.

I Dare You

Whether or not the fun dare is completed, you can easily transition to the real dare by saying, "Actually, what I really dare you to do is have a conversation with *me*." It's best if you choose something you want to have a conversation about, and make it something that easily connects to your faith in Jesus. So you might say, "I dare you to have a conversation with me about…" Simply fill in whatever it is you want to talk about. Here are some easy things you'll both be able to talk about that you can likely connect to your faith, the church, the Scriptures, or Jesus:

- Best memories
- Favorite books
- Favorite activities
- Greatest sacrifice
- Biggest challenges
- Favorite historical person or event

Whatever you choose to talk about, give some thought ahead of time to how you will connect it to your faith. For example, if you want to talk about your favorite books, I hope you would rank the Bible at the top. And if that's the case, be prepared to talk about it. Likewise, if you want to have a conversation about favorite persons or historical events, I hope you will talk about Jesus or His resurrection.

Of course, you can always be direct and say "I dare you to have a conversation with me about Jesus." Here are some of the other direct things you could dare someone to talk with you about:

- The Bible
- Church
- God
- The Holy Spirit

Again, whatever you choose to talk about, give some thought as to how you will talk about it, and what kinds of questions you might ask to help support the conversation.

If the person takes you up on your dare, remember the Holy Spirit is at work in the midst of that conversation. Remember, too, that having a conversation involves two-way communication. You shouldn't be doing all the talking. The best way to approach a conversation is to ask what his or her thoughts are on the topic. Listen to the response carefully for clues on how the Holy Spirit is already working in the other person's life. Here are some general questions you could ask that may help steer your conversation:

- What do you think about (the topic)?
- What makes you feel that way?

- What has your best or most memorable experience been with (the topic)?

Next Steps

Whether you feel the conversation went well or not, there are a few steps you can take to value the person you talked with and further their journey towards the Cross:

- Sincerely thank the person for taking you up on your dare. Let him or her know how much you appreciate the willingness to interact with you.
- If you talked about church, invite the person to church. If you talked about the Bible, invite the person to read your favorite book or chapter in the Bible and share his or her thoughts.
- Check in with him or her over the next few days. See if there are any additional thoughts to discuss.

- Have more conversations! Don't let the occasion of "the dare" be the end of your conversations. It usually takes several conversations for a person to gain faith in Jesus. Keep talking with whomever you've talked to.

---

1 William Fay, *Share Jesus Without Fear* (Nashville: Broadman & Holman Publishers, 1999), 12.
2 Proverbs 12:10; Exodus 23:12; Deuteronomy 25:4.
3 Matthew 6:26; Luke 12:6, 24.
4 Colossians 4:6 NIV
5 See Luke 12:12.
6 John 15:26; John 16:8.
7 Leon Morris, *The Gospel of John*, New International Commentary on the New Testament. Accordance electronic ed. (Grand Rapids: Eerdmans, 1995), 607.
8 Michael Green, *One to One: How to Share Your Faith With a Friend* (Nashville: Moorings, 1995), 12.

I

DARE

YOU

6
...to pray with us.
David Freeland

"Hey, would you like to pray with us?"

That was the question that sparked a movement. It all began when two students, Kaylee and Kenzie, dared to be who God was calling them to be on their school campus. It broke their hearts to simply sit back and do nothing as they watched depression, hopelessness, and drugs have a crushing effect on the lives of their fellow students. Kaylee and Kenzie decided to show the light of Jesus to their peers without fear. Filled with love and compassion for the students on their school campus, they started meeting together every morning in front of their school to pray. Desperate to see God move, they started asking other students the question, "Hey, would you like to pray with us?"

What started with only two students has now grown to more than 40 students praying daily for God to move on their school campus. They've named their group The Prayer Circle, and everyday they pray for the principal, administrators, teachers, and their fellow students. They are also praying for God to open doors and provide opportunities for them to share Jesus with others. The Prayer Circle has also built momentum for the school's Christian Club. They are witnessing change take place on their campus as they pray together.

When asked what changes have taken place in their school, Audree, a friend of Kaylee and Kenzie, said, "I have seen change! There has been a shift in the mood of students. It seems that everyone on our campus is happier. I know it's because the hope of Jesus is changing our school." Her desire and prayer is to see the group expand; to see more people begin to pray and be involved. Audree believes, "Revival will happen through this, which will lead to an awakening of the Gospel in our school of 1,250 students. It will heal our community."

This movement reminds me of a similar one that began in 1990 called "See You At The Pole." Ten students gathered together around their school's flagpole to pray for their school campus. Little did they know that twenty years later millions of students would gather at flagpoles on school campuses all around the world; it happens at 7am on the fourth Wednesday of September every year!

When people come together to faithfully and diligently pray and seek God, God begins to move. What if this kind of movement could start in your school, and what if you could be part of it? In this chapter you will be challenged to dare a friend to pray with you and other Christians on your campus. See You At The Pole is a perfect time to give this dare, but you can really dare your friend any time you're gathering with others to pray. When they ask, "What do you dare me to do?" you reply, "I dare you to pray with us."

Of course, you may not have a regular gathering for prayer at your school. In that case, start one! It doesn't have to be complicated, it just has to be consistent. Get together with other Christians and see when a convenient time would be each day, week, or month, to gather together for prayer at school. Set an appointment together and faithfully keep it!

Gospel-Centered

In Matthew 18:19-20, Jesus said, "Again, truly I tell you that if two of you on earth agree about anything they ask for, it will be done for them by my Father in heaven. For where two or three gather in my name, there am I with them."[1] When two or more people come together and pray, Jesus is there! That means Jesus is actually present on our school campus every time we gather with another believer in the name Jesus. If for no other reason, we should take advantage of the opportunity to pray together because it brings Christ onto our campus! That also means every time you dare your friends to join your group in prayer, you're inviting them to encounter Jesus, whether they realize it or not. It's no wonder Kaylee and Kenzie's group took off so fast—Christ was present, and every person invited into the prayer group had an encounter with Jesus in one way or another.

Spirit-Empowered

Because Jesus is with you, you will sense the power of the Holy Spirit leading and guiding you as you pray. The Holy Spirit will begin to reveal particular things you should pray for that will touch the hearts of your friends, so listen closely to the Spirit's leading. As your friends hear your heartfelt prayers, they will begin to experience the Holy Spirit speaking to them, as well. Their hearts will soften as the Holy Spirit gives you the right things to pray and to say. The experience of the Holy Spirit will plant seeds of trust and faith in your friends' hearts, and will convict them of sin, God's righteousness, and of His judgment.[2]

Personally Responsible for the Mission of God

When Kaylee and Kenzie started The Prayer Circle, they didn't realize how fast it would grow or the effect it would have on their school, but they did know the group wouldn't grow unless they began to invite people to pray with them. They took personal responsibility for inviting others to join them, and it paid off in a big way. Better yet, because Christ was present when the group gathered for prayer, they had also unknowingly taken personal responsibility for introducing those people to Jesus. You should pray *for* your friends, but if you really want to see God move in their lives, take personal responsibility and pray *with* your friends by daring them to join your prayer group.

Have Some Fun

When you wear your "I Dare You" t-shirt in public, you're bound to have a few conversations, and specifically to be asked, "What do you dare me to do?" Before you get to the serious dare, have a little fun. When someone asks you the question, dare them to do the mannequin challenge. The mannequin challenge consists of a person or group of people freezing in dramatic or often difficult-to-maintain poses, acting like literal mannequins, and usually a camera captures it all by panning around the room.[3]

Challenge your friend to strike a difficult pose and hold it for two minutes. Better yet, give this challenge to an entire group, or challenge your friend to gather a group together for the pose. One great topic to create a pose on is the concept of "team." You can challenge the group to do a "team" mannequin challenge. If your friend is alone, or if doing a group pose is not possible, challenge them to create a "team" pose all on their own. Here are some ideas if you want to get specific:

- Create a huddle
- Take a knee together
- Link arms
- Invent a unique handshake
- Make a human pyramid

These are just some ideas, but try to create your own! Make sure you capture the moment and share it on social media with the hashtag #IDareYou.

I Dare You

Whether or not the fun dare is successful, thank your friend, or group of friends, for participating and have a good laugh. Then move on to the real dare by saying something like this: "That took guts! You came together for this dare to create a "team" pose, but that's not the real dare. I really dare you to join *our* team, to pray with us…" Get specific and invite your friends to the next prayer gathering. Give them the time and place, write it down, send them a text, remind them. If you're with a group of Christian friends, or fellow Campus Missionaries, you can even pray as a group at that moment. Share why you think prayer is important, and what you think it could do for your school and for your community. Even if they don't believe in God, you can still invite them to pray with you. Encourage them to give it a try and to see what happens.

Next Steps

After you've invited your friend to join your group for prayer, follow up with them:

- Pray immediately if appropriate. Why wait?
- Keep inviting!
    - Write down your friends' names and cell numbers so you can remind them. Send out a text the day before the prayer group.
    - If your friends reject the idea, thank them for listening. Periodically invite them to join your group over the coming weeks.
    - Challenge your friends to bring other people along.
    - Consider making flyers or cards to invite more people to your prayer group.
- In the prayer group:
    - Pray for each other's needs
    - Pray for your school
        - For its safety
        - For the leadership
        - For the students
        - For opportunities to present the Gospel.

- Have a follow-up discussion:
    - o Ask how your friends how they felt during the time that you prayed together.
    - o Did God speak to them? What did God say, or what did they sense God saying or doing?
    - o Ask if there is anything you can be praying for in particular this week for them.
    - o Ask if they would like to come again.
- What's next? Invite your friends to your Youth Group or host a follow up event outside of school. Connect your new prayer partners with the Body of Christ in the local church.

There are many great resources to help you start a prayer group movement at your school. Here are a few websites to get you started:

- Youth Alive® Prayer Zone Partners: www.yausa.com/pzp
- Claim Your Campus: www.claimyourcampus.com
- See You At The Pole: www.syatp.com.

---

[1] NIV

[2] John 16:8

[3] https://www.bustle.com/articles/193834-where-did-the-mannequin-challenge-come-from-a-look-into-the-meme-sweeping-the-nation

7
...to read the Bible with me.
Jessica Riner

When I was in 12th grade I took an art class hoping for an easy "A." Little did I know it would require so much effort on my part. It was definitely a lot more work than coloring and creating smiley faces, which are my personal favorites to draw. Art class provided a time for great conversations. We could chat about anything while we were creating our work.

On an average day there were four of us sitting at my table, two guys and two girls. The guys had grown up attending a Catholic church. The other girl sitting at my table did not go to church anywhere, as far as I knew. And then you had me, who attended the local Assembly of God church. My friends knew I was a Christian because of the stand I had taken to follow Jesus. I also carried my Bible with me at school on most days.

One day in class the girl asked me about a scripture verse and what it meant. She had heard something on the news that referenced the Bible and wanted to know more. Together we found the verse, read it and talked about what it meant. I can't recall the specific verse we discussed that day in Art Class, however, I do remember what happened over the next few weeks. I invited her to go to church with me. She began coming and within a few weeks she had committed her life to Jesus. Her journey to Christ first began with us reading a Bible verse together and discussing what it meant.

My friend's story reminds me of a passage of scripture found in Acts 8:26-40. An Ethiopian eunuch was reading a few scripture verses from the book of Isaiah. He asked Philip to explain what those verses meant. Philip gave insight to the meaning of the verses and shared the good news of Jesus with his new friend. The Ethiopian decided to get baptized immediately!

Reading the Scriptures opened the Ethiopian's mind to having faith in Jesus. My friend also opened up her mind to receive faith after reading a Scripture verse with me. Reading the Word of God has the power to change lives!

In this chapter, you will be challenged to dare a friend to read the Bible with you over the next few days or weeks. The challenge for you is not just to *read*, but to *discuss* what you read with your friend. As you both share insights on what you've read, you'll have great opportunities to talk about your faith in Jesus. When you wear the *I Dare You* t-shirt and someone asks you, "What do you dare me to do?" don't be afraid to ask them to read and discuss the Bible with you. A great place to begin is to ask them to read the Gospel of John with you.

Gospel-Centered

The Gospel of John is the personal eyewitness account of Jesus' life through the eyes of one of the disciples, John. He stated his purpose for writing in chapter 20, verse 31, "that you may believe that Jesus is the Messiah, the Son of God, and that by believing you may have life in his name."[1] John's Gospel is centered around Jesus Christ, the Messiah who takes away the sins of the whole world. His entire book focuses on the life of Jesus.

John calls for people to believe in Jesus as the Savior of the world and the Son of God. He is calling out for people everywhere to receive eternal life that comes through the death and resurrection of Jesus Christ (3:16-17).[2] When you and your friend begin reading and discussing the Gospel of John together, your friend will also be challenged to believe in Jesus.

Spirit-Empowered

The Holy Spirit speaks to us through the Word of God. When we read the Bible our hearts are exposed to the truth of the good news of Jesus Christ. As you read the Gospel of John together, the Holy Spirit will work in both of you. He will work in you by helping you know what to say to answer questions your friend may ask. The Spirit will also work in the heart of your friend, to convict him or her of sin and bring a realization of who Jesus is. The Holy Spirit will be drawing your friend towards a personal relationship with Jesus.

Hebrews 4:12 tells us the Word of God is living and active. It is able to examine and convict those who read it. Isaiah 55:11 tells us God's Word will not return to us empty, but will accomplish God's desires, and achieve the purposes God has for it. The Holy Spirit will help you have anointed and deep faith conversations with your classmates through this dare to read the Gospel of John.

Personally Responsible for the Mission of God

John stresses the purpose of his Gospel—that we might believe (20:31). The word "believe" has two meanings; "to begin to believe" and "to continue to believe."[3] We need to put our faith in Jesus and encourage others to do the same. It is our personal responsibility. John's life mission was to point people to the cross. Our mission is also to reach out to the lost both at school and at home and encourage them to believe in Jesus.

Have Some Fun

I would venture to say most people love the adrenaline rush of a dare. As people see you wearing the *I Dare You* t-shirt they will read those words. Some will ask, "What do you dare me to do?" Be prepared to have a good time and give out dares to your friends.

Tongue twisters can be a lot of fun, so memorize a few and have them ready. Here are some you can try: *She sells seashells by the seashore*, or *six slippery snails, slid slowly seaward*, or *how much wood would a woodchuck chuck if a woodchuck could chuck wood?*. When you're asked for a dare, say, "I dare you to repeat this tongue twister five times, out loud, as fast as you can." Have your friends repeat it to you or to a group of friends. The point is to break the ice and have fun with the dare.

I Dare You

If your friend accepts the fun dare you'll be laughing together in no time. Maybe some others will join in and try the fun dare, too. Now transition the conversation by saying something like, "I have another dare for you, and this one is actually the real dare. I dare you to read the Bible with me." Try to get your friend to begin to read the Gospel of John and talk about it with you over the next few days.

Your friend may come back with the question, "Why?" Be ready with your answer. Share that the words of the Bible have changed your own life. The Bible gives practical advice, helps us have self-control, change habits we would like to overcome, and make good decisions. Most of all, reading the Bible helps us learn the truth about Jesus.

Some people believe the Bible is hard to understand, some think it is boring, and others believe it is too time consuming. Helping your friend see the value in reading the Bible is important.

Once your friend agrees to read the Bible with you, set a time table; read it over the next 7 days, 10 days, or 21 days. The Gospel of John has 21 chapters. If you choose the 7 days, you would be reading three chapters a day and discussing it with your friend. Should you choose 10 days, you'll read two chapters a day until the last day. Finally, if you choose 21 days, you would be reading and discussing one chapter each day. Pick the best option depending on the time of year and your class schedule. Sometimes reading things slower and being able to digest it is best.

The lunch table is a great place for the discussion. Ask your friends to join you at your table. This could easily develop into more Bible discussions throughout the year over lunch. However, if lunch doesn't seem like the best time, you can always chat before or after school.

Be ready to share your thoughts on the chapter you read. Ask good questions to get the conversation flowing. The important thing to remember is that you need to allow your friend to share honest thoughts and ask questions without feeling like he or she will be judged harshly for their opinions.

Here are some good questions to get you going:

- What stuck out to you the most from your Bible reading today?
- What new thing did you learn from these verses?
- Which verse meant the most to you today? Why?
- What did you think about _____? (Fill in the blank with a topic from that day's reading.)
- What challenged you?
- Do you have any questions from what you read? If you don't know the answer it's ok to say, "That is a great question, but I am not sure I know the answer. Let me research it some and get back to you tomorrow." Be willing to ask your youth pastor or another Christian leader for advice on the subject.

Never underestimate the power of the Holy Spirit to speak to your friend directly as he or she is reading through the Gospel of John with you. This dare, when accepted, opens the door for the Holy Spirit to reveal the truth about Jesus and our need for a personal relationship with God. The Bible is God's Word and it speaks life and truth to us every time we read it.

Next Steps

Reading the Gospel of John takes a commitment from both you and your friends. Your friends may or may not complete the entire book. Don't take it personally if they don't make it all the way; instead, choose to add value to your friends.

Here are a few steps to take to encourage them in their journey of faith to Jesus:

- Genuinely thank them for the time they took to complete any part of your dare.
- Never make your friends feel less respected if they don't complete the dare.
- Continue to build a friendship with those you encountered for this dare. Friendship opens the door for future conversations about God, the Bible, and Jesus, as the Son of God.

---

[1] NIV.

[2] *Faithlife Study Bible*, ed. John D. Barry, Logos Bible Software (Lexham Press: 2016), notes from John 20:31.

[3] *Evangelical Commentary on the Bible*, ed. Walter Elwell, Logos Bible Software, (Baker Bytes/Baker Publishing Group: 1995), NIV margin notes on John 20:31.

I
DARE
YOU

8

...to list your blessings.
Kent Hulbert

A blessing is defined as "a thing conducive to happiness or welfare."[1] What has made your life happy? Can you begin to make a list of ways that God has blessed your life? We don't often think of the tough times or bad situations we've gone through as blessings; they don't typically make it onto the list. Why would they? The pain from the bad moments can seem overwhelming and never-ending. How could you ever find something good in those moments that are shameful, hurtful, embarrassing? Is it possible to find something to be grateful for in all that mess? I have discovered the answer is...YES!

I came across a true story that has served as a strong reminder for me that some of the worst moments can be turned into blessings. A century ago, the people of Coffee County, Alabama dedicated a unique statue honoring the Mexican boll weevil. Why would anyone build a monument to a bug?

In 1910 boll weevils began to destroy the major crop of Coffee County—Cotton. Cotton farming had been the main crop in the south for decades, but now the entire community was struggling to make ends meet due to this destructive bug. In their fight to survive, the farmers planted other types of other crops, including peanuts. It didn't take long for the farmers to discover they could be just as well-off, if not more so, farming peanuts instead of cotton. In fact, by 1917 Coffee County had harvested the largest peanut crop in the nation![2]

Just two years later, during this time of peanut prosperity, they built and erected the statue. The inscription on the statue reads: "In profound appreciation of the boll weevil and what it has done as the Herald of Prosperity, this monument was erected by the citizens of Enterprise,

Coffee County, Alabama." Although the boll weevil caused a disaster to the cotton crop, the forced switch to growing peanuts ended up being a great blessing to the farming industry and the surrounding community. The gratitude felt for the boll weevil was so important to the town that it demonstrated its thankfulness by creating the world's first and only memorial honoring a bug.[3]

Thankfulness is also critical to a follower of Jesus. Check out Colossians 2:6-7, "And now, just as you accepted Christ Jesus as your Lord, you must continue to follow Him. Let your roots grow down into him, and let your lives be built on him. Then your faith will grow strong in the truth you were taught, and you will overflow with thankfulness."[4] Paul used two images in that passage: "roots" like a plant or tree, and "built-on" like a building with a proper foundation. Both images paint a picture of how giving thanks strengthens us. Thanksgiving also helps us stay alert to the enemy and sensitive to God's work in us. Colossians 4:2 reads, "Devote yourselves to prayer with an alert mind and a thankful heart."[5] Thanksgiving is essential to our everyday walk and shouldn't be limited to a holiday or a few select moments of the year.

Go ahead and list some of your blessings. Think of the big things you are thankful for, but also consider the small blessings of life we tend to take for granted (the air we breathe, the food we eat, etc.). As you begin to make your list, take into account the tough times you have gone through. We wouldn't normally think of being grateful for the things that have caused us pain. Yet, James wrote that we should count trials and troubles of many kinds as "all joy," because it leads us into a stronger faith through perseverance.[6] God can turn those hurtful experiences into a time of growth that otherwise may never have happened. So what are your blessings? What are you thankful for?

In this chapter you will be challenged to help people take a moment to reflect and find the blessings in their lives; even those who may not think they have any. When they ask, "What do you dare me to do?" you reply, "I dare you to list your blessings…what are you thankful for?" As you dare others to list their blessings, you can even help them realize that God can give the "boll weevils" in life a purpose too!

Gospel-Centered

Our perspective, how we view things, strongly determines what we consider to be a blessing. The Bible teaches that so many of the everyday things we experience are actually blessings from God. We tend to take these things for granted, as though God had nothing to do with them, but this is a subtle deception. That's why James, the brother of Jesus, warned and taught us, "Don't be deceived, my dear brothers and sisters. Every good and perfect gift is from above, coming down from the Father of the heavenly lights, who does not change like shifting shadows."[7] When you challenge others to list their blessings, you are really challenging them to list the things God has blessed them with, whether they realize it or not.

We all have something to be grateful and thankful for: Jesus paid for our sin with his life. He did so regardless of whether people accept, reject, deny, or ridicule Him. The news becomes even better. As we walk with Jesus, He can turn all things—even the bad things—to our good. Romans 8:28 states, "And we know that God causes everything to work together for the good of those who love God and are called according to his purpose for them."[8] God turns our difficulties and troubles into blessings.

Spirit-Empowered

Take some time to ask the Holy Spirit to show you—remind you—of the ways God is with you and how He has blessed you. It takes humility to realize that even the simplest of good things in our lives comes from God, and not from our own power. That kind of humility and meekness is a fruit of the Holy Spirit's work in us.[9] Ask the Holy Spirit to help you make a list of what you are thankful for, including the simple things and the difficult challenges. When you challenge others to list their blessings, challenge them to list the simple things, as well. When you do, you'll create space for the Holy Spirit to awaken the same humble realization in them—that so many of the blessings in our lives are beyond our control and come from our Creator.

Personally Responsible for the Mission of God

Giving thanks for our blessings helps us to stay ready to share the Gospel and stay focused on God's mission. Colossians 4:2-6 reads:

Devote yourselves to prayer with an alert mind and a thankful heart. Pray for us, too, that God will give us many opportunities to speak about his mysterious plan concerning Christ. That is why I am here in chains. Pray that I will proclaim this message as clearly as I should. Live wisely among those who are not believers, and make the most of every opportunity. Let your conversation be gracious and attractive so that you will have the right response for everyone.[10]

A thankful heart helps you to proclaim the Gospel clearly, to live wisely around those who don't know Jesus, to make the most of every moment, and it helps your conversations draw people toward Jesus.

God has entrusted us to share His great love with others. A thankful heart makes you more sensitive to God's work in you, and also to God's desire to save all people. Be thankful that He has placed you in your school, in your community, and in your home. Let that thankfulness flow out of you as you take personal responsibility and challenge others to consider their own blessings from God.

Have Some Fun

As always, it's good to break the ice with a fun dare before you get to the serious dare. You can always come up with your own dares to break the ice, but here is an easy and fun idea: challenge the person who asks "what do you dare me to do?" to shake hands and say "thank you" to five random people. Have fun with it.

I Dare You

You can easily transition to the serious dare by saying, "They are probably wondering why you are so thankful. But I actually have another, more serious dare for you. I dare you to list the blessings in your life. What do you have to be thankful for?" Be prepared for some of the standard responses such as thankfulness for a person, an event in life, or things your friend owns. Follow up by asking, "What makes you thankful for that? What makes it meaningful?" Take time to hear the whole story of why those things are so meaningful; try to understand why they are special or important.

Listen to the Holy Spirit as you have the conversation, looking for opportunities to connect those blessings to God and the Gospel. For example, if your friend is thankful for a person, you can talk about the people who are meaningful in your life. Perhaps that would be the person who led you to Jesus, or Jesus, Himself. If your friend expresses gratefulness for a certain event in life, you can share thankfulness for circumstances or events that had special spiritual significance for you.

Most people won't list the simple, everyday things we are given in life as blessings: the air we breathe, the clothes on our backs, the food we have to eat, the abilities we have within our own physical bodies. You can push the conversation further towards God by listing out some of these simple blessings. Challenge your friend to list some simple things. Have a discussion about where these simple blessings come from and what you believe about it.

When you feel comfortable, ask if your friend has experienced any difficulties or suffering in life that can now be viewed as bringing blessings. Simply ask, "Have you ever experienced a situation that was difficult at the time, but you ended up being thankful for in the long run?" Be prepared to share a story of your own. This may be a foreign concept to your friend, and it might be a perfect opportunity to share James 1:2-4, emphasizing how your faith makes it possible for you to be thankful for the times in life you've suffered. Transition the conversation towards Jesus by discussing His suffering and why you are thankful for it. Ask for your friend's thoughts.

Next Steps

Below are a few ideas to continue the conversations:

- Always thank your friends for taking you up on the dare. Let them know how much you appreciate their willingness to interact with you and their openness to talk.
- Invite them to church. Have a discussion about how church is a blessing in your life that you'd like to share.
- Encourage them to keep adding to their list of blessings. Connect over lunch in a few days to talk about the new things that have been discovered.
- Have more conversations! Don't let the occasion of "the dare" be the end of your conversations. It usually takes several conversations for a person to gain faith in Jesus. Keep talking with whomever you've talked to.

---

1 "Blessing." Merriam-Webster.com. Accessed February 14, 2017. https://www.merriam-webster.com/dictionary/blessing.
2 Ben Berntson, "Boll Weevil Monument," in *Encyclopedia of Alabama* (Alabama Humanities Foundation: 2016), http://www.encyclopediaofalabama.org/article/h-2384. Accessed March 16, 2017.
3 Ibid.
4 NLT
5 NLT
6 James 1:2-4
7 James 1:16-17 NIV
8 NLT
9 Galatians 5:22-23
10 NLT

I DARE YOU

9
...to serve with me.
Jason Forsman

"Please stop calling me." That's what I was thinking after hearing my phone ring for the second or third time early one morning. I had been working late the night before and did *not* want to get out of bed that morning. I finally rolled over and answered the phone, my eyes still too blurry to read who it was.

"Jason, are you still in bed?" It was Dennis. Dennis Whaley was calling me, again, for who knew what. I loved Dennis and his whole family because they had always accepted me and loved me, even when they knew I wasn't living the kind of lifestyle I should have been. But, I was very tired.

"Hey, Dennis, no, I'm awake. What's up?"

"Jason, it's move-in day at Evangel. I need you to come help people carry in their stuff. I'll see you in 20 minutes."

It was another one of Dennis' events for which he "needed" my help. He was constantly asking me to come help with this, or serve here, or teach this class. It didn't matter how many times I turned him down or didn't follow through all the way, he still asked me to come serve beside him. I hated it and loved it at the same time. I learned two things from working side by side with Dennis: how to love people the way God loves us, and how to let God love me the way He wants to. Dennis was a perfect example of someone with the heart of a servant. Every time he invited me to serve beside him, it had a deep and lasting impact on my life.

Serving others changes us; it moves us past self-centeredness and places value on those around us. Not only that, but loving and serving others is a Biblical mandate. 1 Peter 4:8-10, 11b states:

Above all, keep loving one another earnestly, since love covers a multitude of sins. Show hospitality to one another without grumbling. As each has received a gift, use it to serve one another, as good stewards of God's varied grace…whoever serves, as one who serves by the strength that God supplies—in order that in everything God may be glorified through Jesus Christ.[1]

God is glorified when we serve through His strength. What does that mean? It means to truly serve we have to put others first. It's not in our normal nature to put someone else first, which is why we must rely on God's strength to get it right. If we do this, we will demonstrate Christ's love in a practical and helpful way, and God will be glorified. Bringing a friend alongside us as we serve is a great way to open the door to faith in his or her life.

In this chapter you'll be challenged to dare a friend to serve others with you. Start a journey with your friend and see where it leads. Of course, this is also a challenge for you, because you will have to serve others, as well. When your friend says, "What do you dare me to do?" you reply, "I dare you to serve alongside me."

Gospel-Centered

Jesus spent a large amount of time with his disciples serving others. It was a significant part of His method for training them; He invited them to walk with Him when He healed, fed, taught, and served the people around Him. He was focused on the needs of others, and in doing so, He taught his disciples to do the same. He was demonstrating and teaching what was at the core of his very nature; Jesus was a servant. His ultimate service for all of us was on the Cross. That's why He said, "The Son of Man came not to be served, but to serve, and to give His life as a ransom for many."[2] When Jesus invited His disciples to serve alongside Him, He was teaching them how to be like He was. When you serve alongside your friend, you'll also be demonstrating the nature of Christ and you'll have the opportunity to talk about who Jesus is.

Spirit-Empowered

Dennis never complained. He always served everyone around him with a smile. Often, when I asked him how he did it, he'd tell me it was only because of the Holy Spirit in his life. He was absolutely correct; we can't serve in God's strength without the Holy Spirit, it's just not in our nature. It's the Holy Spirit's presence in our lives that grows the fruit of the Spirit: love, joy, peace, patience, kindness, goodness, faithfulness, gentleness, and self-control.[3] As you serve alongside your friend the Holy Spirit will empower you, helping you serve in God's strength, demonstrating the true nature of Christ through the fruit of the Spirit.

Serving others together may seem like a weak or ineffective way to share Jesus, but the opposite is actually true: it is in weakness and service that the Holy Spirit's power is made known to our friends. The Apostle Paul knew this and lived it out intentionally. By the most reliable accounts, Paul was a well-educated, intellectually powerful speaker who served as an international ambassador for Christ.[4] Yet, in spite of his abilities, he frequently chose to serve others in weakness so that the Holy Spirit's power could be the main factor in convincing them to believe in Jesus. He wrote, "God's Spirit and God's power did it, which made it clear that your life of faith is a response to God's power, not to some fancy mental or emotional footwork by me or anyone else."[5] The same thing will happen when you serve alongside your friend in Christ-like humility—the Holy Spirit will clearly and persuasively draw him to faith in Jesus.

Personally Responsible for the Mission of God

Some of the most meaningful things about serving alongside my friend Dennis were the conversations we had during those times. As we served side-by-side, he would talk with me about my life. Dennis took personal responsibility to engage me in conversations, and those conversations often came around to faith. You must do the same thing Dennis did. While the Holy Spirit draws your friend toward faith in Jesus as you serve together, you must also speak the name of Jesus and talk about your faith in Him. That's why Paul wrote, "For everyone who calls on the name of the Lord will be saved. But how can they call on Him they have not believed in? And how can they believe without hearing about Him? And how can they hear without a preacher?"[6] Be that preacher. Take personal responsibility. Have a conversation, take an interest in your friend, and listen for opportunities to talk about Christ as the true servant who gave Himself for us on the Cross.

Have Some Fun

Before you move into the serious dare of serving together, have some fun. Do you know what it means to "pay it forward?" It's what happens when a person receives a blessing, or benefits from a good deed, and then uses that blessing to benefit someone other than the person who originally blessed him. Dare a friend to "pay it forward" in one of the following ways:

- Give him $5 and tell him you dare him to pay it forward by giving it to someone else or buying someone a meal.
- A much less costly way is to dare him to look around for someone who needs a hand and then go help.
- If there's no one around for your friend to help, fall down dramatically and dare him to help you up. You might look like a goofball, but it will, at least, break the ice. You could also dare him to tell you about the last time he helped someone and didn't expect anything in return.

I Dare You

Once the conversation moves beyond the fun dare, transition by telling him about a time when you served someone or a group of people and how it made you feel. Let him know about an upcoming opportunity you have to serve, or ask him if he has any ideas for how to serve in the community. Then give the dare by saying, "I dare you to serve alongside me. Let's go do this together." If he says yes, follow through and make it happen. If he says no, don't be discouraged. Simply dare your friend, again, when another opportunity comes along. If your friend needs a ride, pick him up. Consider serving with a group of friends from your youth group in order to have a greater influence. You'll have a blast serving together, and your friend will see God's love in action through you.

A great time to give this dare is during the Thanksgiving or Christmas season, because so many things around us are already pointing to goodwill for all mankind. The whole season is geared toward giving and serving others, with special consideration to those less fortunate. If you don't have any opportunities coming up to serve through your church, consider these easy ways of creating opportunities on your own:

- Put together meals and deliver them to families in need in your community.
- Find an elementary school that would love to have you come in and tutor or read with students.
- Bring hot chocolate or coffee to all the police officers on shift one day, or to all the crossing guards in your city one cold morning, or deliver blankets and hot meals to the homeless.

- Do yard work for those in the community who are unable to do it themselves.

Next Steps

If your friend says yes, take the following actions to ensure a great day of serving together:

- Make sure you are on time.
- Have a well thought out plan for the time of serving. Allow your friend to help plan it with you.
- Plan to have a conversation during the event, as well as afterwards. Think through some questions you can ask to start a conversation.
- Get some food and talk together about your feelings and reactions to the day. Give your friend a lot of room to talk.
- When it's your turn to talk about the day, be sure to talk about how Jesus is your ultimate motivation for serving.

Once you've spent time with him, let him know some of other ways he is welcome to serve with you, your youth group, or your group of Christian friends:

- Invite him to your next youth group meeting or service.
- Let him know about upcoming events where you can serve together, again.
- Find out if there are any ways you can serve him. If there are any outstanding needs in his life, you and your friends need to work together to find a way to help.

Above all else, keep looking for opportunities to serve and invite your friends to join you. Paul said, "In your relationships with one another, have the same mindset as Christ Jesus...he made himself nothing by taking the very nature of a servant..."[7] Every time you serve others (and every time you serve together) you are setting an example of Jesus' love, and by also talking about Jesus, you are pointing them directly to the cross.

---

[1] ESV
[2] Mark 10:45, Matthew 20:27 ESV
[3] Galatians 5:22-23
[4] Hanz Deiter Betz, "PAUL," in *The Anchor Yale Bible Dictionary*, ed. David Noel Freedman (New York: Doubleday, 1992), 5:187.
[5] 1 Corinthians 2:4–5 The Message
[6] Romans 10:13–14 HCSB
[7] Philippians 2:5, 7a NIV

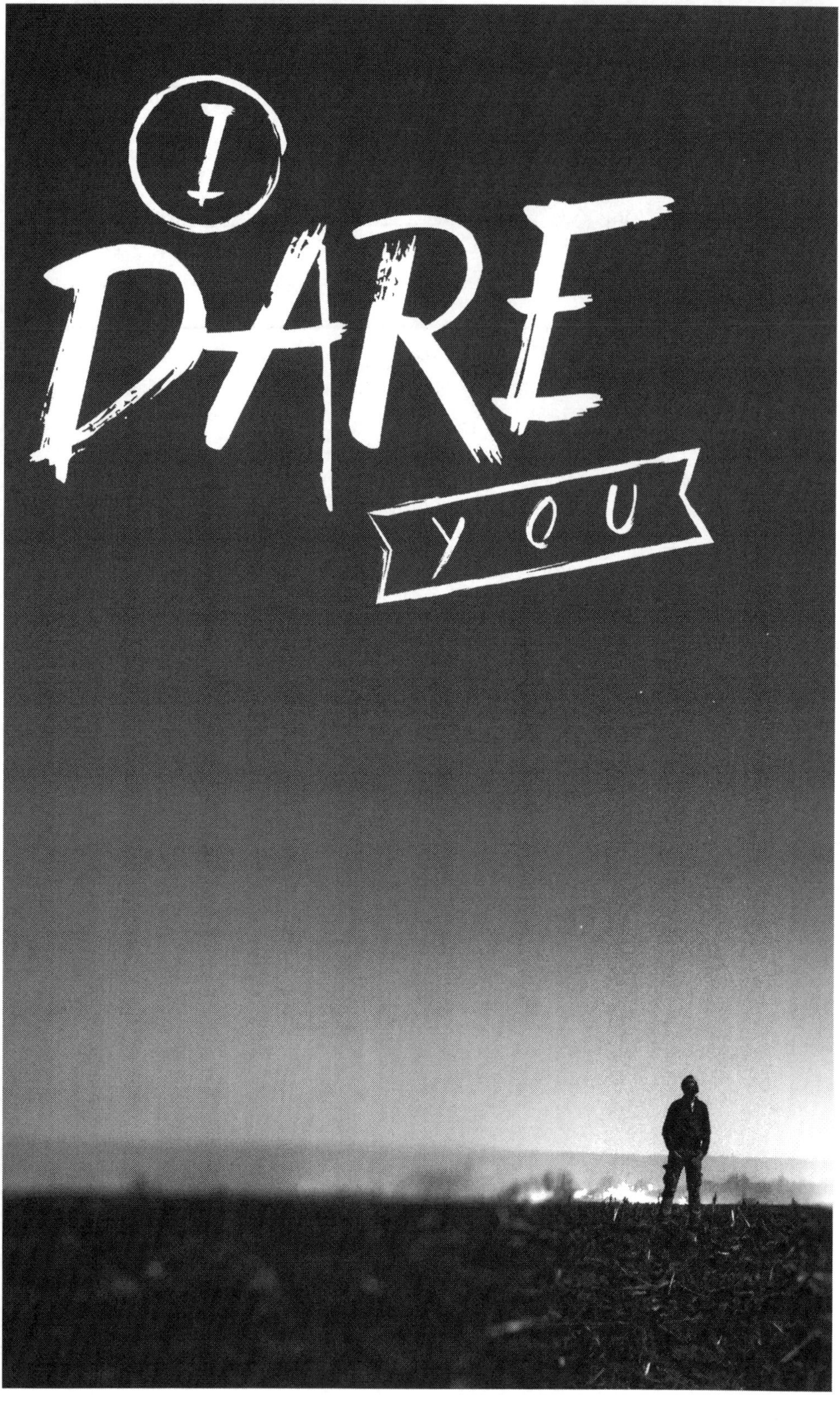
I
DARE
YOU

10
...to change.
Ben Russell

"Isn't your Dad a preacher?" If I had a penny for every time I heard that during my school years, I would be a very wealthy man. I went to high school in a relatively small town where my Dad was pretty well known as one of the local pastors. It seemed like I had been asked that question hundreds of times, although this time felt a little different. This question came from someone I considered a friend. I had not known her very long, but she was a friend, nonetheless. Her name was Rachel. She was dating a very good friend of mine that I played ball with, so I was really curious to see where this conversation might go. There was only one way to find out.

"Yes, he is," I replied back to her.

She followed up by asking, "So you are probably a pretty churchy person?"

I wasn't 100% sure how to answer, although I had a pretty decent idea of what she meant. "Yeah, I am a Christian, if that's what you mean."

Rachel went on to say her life was in a difficult place and, though she was not attending church at the time, she remembered what it was like growing up in church and having a relationship with Jesus. Rachel was crying out for help at school, and she didn't care who was around. She was desperate, and I knew this conversation would be different.

I went on to explain that I was far from perfect, that I had struggles like every other teenager, but I also had a relationship with God. It wasn't an easy conversation, but she had approached me and really needed someone to talk to about God. The door had opened, so I walked through it. I'm glad I did. Rachel rededicated her life to Christ a couple weeks later in her church! To my knowledge she is still serving the Lord today. Rachel really wanted to change, and she knew she had to turn her life over to God for change to happen.

We don't often realize it, but many people around us are also desperate for change; we just have to open our eyes and see it. To *change* means to become different or become altered, modified.[1] Some people are looking for an entire life change, while others would only change a few things. In this chapter you are going to be challenged to dare others to identify one thing in their lives they would like change, and to consider how God could help them change it. You can give this dare at any time, but New Year's is an easy time to do it because so many people are already thinking about things they want to change by making New Year's resolutions. When your friend asks, "What do you dare me to do?" you reply, "I dare you to name one thing about yourself you'd like to change and have a conversation with me about it."

Gospel-Centered

One great example in the Bible of someone who truly changed was Saul, who was later called Paul.[2] He killed and persecuted Christians, but he had an incredible "change" moment while traveling on the road to Damascus. God verbally spoke to him! Paul changed and began to do so many great things for God—about half of the book of Acts is written about him! He went on to write a good portion of the New Testament. The Gospel changed Saul into Paul. The Gospel changes us, as well. Never think someone can't change, even if it's the "roughest" person in your school or a family member who seems closed off to anything regarding God. Think about Paul—the person who persecuted the church but went on to become an incredible leader and follower of Christ.

Spirit-Empowered

John 14:26 says, "But the Advocate, the Holy Spirit, whom the Father will send in my name, will teach you all things and will remind you of everything I have said to you."[3] Jesus called the Holy Spirit our "advocate," meaning the Spirit is here to help when friends, family, and classmates are trying to change. It is essential that we remember it is by the Spirit's help that change happens in our lives and in the lives of others.

I like the way Pastor Herbert Cooper describes the work of the Holy Spirit in us:

God has more than enough daily bread to sustain you, assurance and support to strengthen you, and the presence of His Spirit to encourage and empower you. No matter where you are in life, if you're battered and broken by life, God can mend you. He can restore you.[4]

If there was ever a "mic drop" moment, that is it! We can change through the power of the Holy Spirit and the work He does in us. When you dare a friend to name one thing they would change, he may name something that can only change through the power of the Holy Spirit. That's good, because you'll have an opportunity to talk about the Holy Spirit, how the Spirit has helped you change, and how the Spirit can help your friend change.

Personally Responsible for the Mission of God

Jesus gave clear instructions to his disciples before He returned to Heaven. He said, "Go into all the world and preach the Good News to everyone."[5] This is called "The Great Commission." If we have been challenged to share the good news, the Gospel, then we have been challenged to do our part to see people around us change. The Great Commission is truly a great responsibility, and it is *our* great responsibility.

Even so, it can be uncomfortable to challenge someone to change. I'll never forget in Jr. High, when I was really trying to witness to a friend, I told him everything that was wrong in his life. Needless to say, my words weren't well received at all. The biggest problem was my approach, but my timing was also bad. I brought it up out of the blue and, if my memory serves me right, I led with something like, "You know, if you died today you probably wouldn't make it to Heaven." Yes, I'll admit, it was a really bad way to start. My heart was in the right place, I just didn't use any wisdom. I was so overwhelmed with my responsibility that I didn't take the time to pray beforehand or to think through the words I would say.

Remember to pray that God would lead you with the right words and the right timing. It doesn't have to be awkward, just be sensitive with the words you say, and when you choose to say them. Challenging my friend to basically change everything about his life was not the right path to take. If I could do it over again, I would dare him to name one thing he'd like to see change in his life, and then I'd ask if we could pray together for the Holy Spirit to help him change that one thing. This simple, yet meaningful conversation can allow God to reveal His power and open the door for your friend to place his full faith in Jesus.

Have Some Fun

It's always important to have a little fun to break the ice before getting to the more serious dare. One great way to introduce the concept of change might be to say, "I dare you to walk up to a complete stranger and ask them if you can give him (or her) your spare change." If the person asks why, tell them to say, "Because change is good." This can lead to some great conversations. Be respectful of everyone you and your friend encounter. Have a good time and a good laugh together.

I Dare You

They say timing is everything, and although I'm not sure who "they" are, it is a very wise statement. Pray the Holy Spirit would nudge you at the right time. When you sense the time is right, you should say, "Actually, I dare you to name one thing about yourself you'd like to change and have a conversation about it." Naturally, your friend will respond with a few questions. The Holy Spirit will lead you in this discussion, but you should prepare yourself ahead of time to think through how the conversation might go.

It's also possible that you could offend your friend by daring him or her to change. Also, *do not* point out the things you think need to change in your friend's life. This dare is not about you judging others; it's about allowing the Holy Spirit to speak to your friend about change. So let the Holy Spirit do the convicting, and let your friend make the decision.

Here are some possibilities of what your friend could ask you, as well as some possible responses:

- What do you mean? *We all have some things about ourselves that we need to change, things we could be doing better. I've personally needed to change a lot, and I continually need to change.*
- What do I need to change? *Well, I've changed my life to try to live more like Jesus, to read the Bible, and to obey God in all I do. That's a big change. What is one thing you would change about yourself to be a better person?*
- Why do I need to change? *Because we all fail, we've all fallen short of the ideal. We all need to strive to change and be more like Jesus.*
- How do I change? *When something needs to change in my life, I pray*

that God would help me through the Holy Spirit. Could we pray together and ask the Holy Spirit to help you?

- Who is going to help me change? *God will help you, and I will help you, too.*

You should also be prepared to share some ways in which you have been challenged to change, and give some testimonies about how the Holy Spirit has helped you to change.

Here are a few more questions for you to ask your friend as the conversation continues:

- What do you need to do to start changing?
- What are some things you need to eliminate in your life in order to change?
- What can I do to help you?
- In what ways could God help you change?
- Can we pray together and ask for God's help?

Next Steps

Make sure this is just the beginning of an ongoing conversation—don't let it end here. God will give you the strength to keep this dare going, and here are some ideas that can help:

- Share a meal with your friend to ask about how the change is going.
- Share some testimonies of what your process of change has been like, or share how you are trying to change currently.
- Encourage them to read the book of Acts so they can read about Paul and how he changed.
- Invite them to attend church with you.
- Give them plenty of encouragement along the way.

---

[1] *Merriam-Webster's Collegiate Dictionary*, 10th ed. (Springfield, MA: Merriam-Webster Incorporated, 1999).
[2] Acts 13:9
[3] John 14:26 NIV
[4] Herbert Cooper, *But God: Changes Everything* (Grand Rapids: Zondervan, 2014), 179-180.
[5] Mark 16:15 NLT

I
DARE
YOU

11
...to love like Jesus.
Wes Sheley

I love February. More than any other month of the year, love seems to be in the air. Actually, it's not love as much as it is the color red; the Valentine's decorations, cards, candy, stuffed animals, and flowers are everywhere! Everyone seems focused on the people they love…or on finding someone to love. The word "love" is everywhere in February, yet love can mean very different things to different people. Our experiences in life determine our understanding of love, and everyone's experiences are different.

Love took on a whole new meaning for my wife and I just five months into our marriage. It was February 2000, and my wife began having physical problems that forced her to go to the doctor. After several days and appointments, my wife and I were back in the doctor's office, waiting for her MRI results to come in. She rested on an exam bed and though it seemed we waited all day, it was actually only an hour before the doctor came in. He had a look on his face that I can only describe as "I hate this part of my job." Just a few months before, my wife and I had made our marriage vows, including "in sickness and in health," and that particular promise was about to be tested with a cruel dose of reality.

The doctor approached the exam bed and grabbed my wife's hand. With a solemn tone he said, "I'm sorry, but you have Multiple Sclerosis."

When the Doctor left the room my wife and I sat in silence for a while. Then we began trying to process what life was going to be like for us; how it was going to change and how we would make it through. That day began a journey for my wife and I—a journey through the years to learn what it means to love each other the way Christ loves us.

Multiple Sclerosis (MS) is a debilitating disease that disrupts the nervous system and causes new problems as time goes on. There have been days when my wife can hardly function, other times she's had to walk with a cane, and sometimes she's even been restricted to a wheel chair. It is during these times I am reminded that we all change, and the woman I married in 1999 is different from the woman I am married to today. I am different, too. We have both learned how to love more deeply, and that we have to choose to love each other daily. We have learned that true love makes it easier to look past our imperfections and serve one another sacrificially. This is the kind of love that Jesus Christ shows each one of us—sacrificial love.

It's always interesting to hear other people's definitions of love, because everyone has a different story and experience that helps define love for them. Some may struggle with love because of betrayal, divorce, hurts, abandonment, or illnesses. Walking with my wife through MS has helped me better understand what love is. The ultimate definition of love is found in the person and actions of Jesus Christ, who said in John 15:13, "Greater love has no one than this: to lay down one's life for one's friends."[1]

One great way to share the Gospel with your friends is to talk about the love of God, which was expressed through Jesus' willing sacrifice of Himself. In this chapter you will be challenged to dare a friend to love like Jesus. When they ask, "What do you dare me to do?" you reply, "I dare you to love like Jesus!"

Gospel-Centered

1 Corinthians 13 is known as the love chapter, and it continuously reminds us what true love is. This chapter gives one of the most eloquent and famous descriptions of love ever written:

> Love is patient, love is kind. It does not envy, it does not boast, it is not proud. It does not dishonor others, it is not self-seeking, it is not easily angered, it keeps no record of wrongs. Love does not delight in evil but rejoices with the truth. It always protects, always trust, always hopes always perseveres. Love never fails.[2]

Love is not just a feeling or an emotion; it is also a choice. The choice is to sacrifice our own self-interest for the benefit of someone else. This is the choice Jesus made when He chose to go to the cross for us. He is the ultimate example of sacrificial love.

Let's replace the word "love" in the same section of Scripture with Jesus' name, and the word "it" with the word "He":

> Jesus is patient, Jesus is kind. He does not envy, He does not boast, He is not proud. He does not dishonor others, He is not self-seeking, He is not easily angered, He keeps no record of wrongs. Jesus does not delight in evil but rejoices with the truth. He always protects, always trust, always hopes, always perseveres. Jesus never fails.

While we can't be perfect in the same way Jesus was perfect, we can imitate Him by loving others sacrificially. So when you dare your friends to love like Jesus, you'll be challenging them to experience sacrificial love, naturally pointing to Christ and opening the door to faith.

Spirit-Empowered

Ultimately, no one can love like Jesus without the help of the Holy Spirit. The Apostle Paul places love first in the list of the fruits of the Holy Spirit. He most likely put it first because the other fruits of the Spirit are dependent on love, and flow from love.[3] He chose the word "fruit" purposefully, because this kind of love is something that grows in our lives like fruit grows on a tree as we allow the Holy Spirit to work in us.

When you dare your friends to love like Christ, you are challenging them to do something that is impossible without the help of the Holy Spirit. That's a good thing, because you can talk to them about how the Holy Spirit helps you to love sacrificially, and how the Holy Spirit can help them do the same. If they take you up on the dare, they'll be opening themselves to a deeper conversation with the Holy Spirit.

Personally Responsible for the Mission of God

Loving my wife sacrificially through the challenges she faces has required me to give the Holy Spirit room to work and to practice love. That is ultimately my personal responsibility; I must choose to love, and in doing so I must allow the Holy Spirit's influence to grow in my life. You must also take personal responsibility to choose to love your friends. You should dare them to love like Jesus, but first make sure you are loving your friends like Jesus does. Taking personal responsibility doesn't just include speaking to them about Christ's sacrificial love; it's equally about demonstrating Christ's sacrificial love. When you take personal responsibility to love first, and talk second, your words become more trustworthy and credible.

Have Some Fun

It's always important to have a little fun before you get to the serious dare. When you wear your t-shirt and someone approaches you and asks you to dare them to do something, ask him to name one family member who means a lot to them (father, mother, brother, sister, grandparents, etc.). When he has chosen that family member, dare him to declare, loud enough for everyone in the area to hear, "I love my _____ (father, mother, brother, sister, grandparents, etc.)!" Have a good time and treat the person gracefully whether he completes the dare or not.

I Dare You

Whether or not he completes the first dare, transition to the real challenge by saying, "Actually, that's not the real dare. What I really dare you to do is to love like Jesus loves." Naturally, there will be questions as to what exactly that means. Simply discuss that the greatest example of love you have discovered is Jesus. Share John 15:13, sharing that there is no greater love than to lay down our life for someone else, and explain that loving like Jesus means sacrificing in a meaningful way for someone else's benefit. You can also share 1 Corinthians 13, the famous love chapter of the Bible we discussed earlier.

Don't let the conversation end there, but continue to push the dare forward by asking your friend to think of a particular person who needs to be loved like Jesus loves – with a love that requires sacrifice. Once he names that person, push the dare in a specific direction by asking, "What is a meaningful sacrifice you could make to love this person?" Help them explore meaningful sacrifice and brainstorm ideas by asking the following questions:

- What does this person need?
- What does this person want from you?
- What would bless this person?

If your friend is still struggling, make some simple suggestions, such as a service project around the person's house, helping with homework, spending time together, a financial gift, a trip or night out together, etc.

An important goal of this dare is to have a meaningful conversation about Jesus, and if the conversation has gotten this far, you've reached that goal. However, you can still take the conversation further towards faith in Christ by discussing the encompassing love that drove Jesus' sacrifice. Romans 5:6-8 is a great passage for this, and I love the way The Message puts it:

> He presented himself for this sacrificial death when we were far too weak and rebellious to do anything to get ourselves ready. And even if we hadn't been so weak, we wouldn't have known what to do anyway. We can understand someone dying for a person worth dying for, and we can understand how someone good and noble could inspire us to selfless sacrifice. But God put his love on the line for us by offering his Son in sacrificial death while we were of no use whatever to him.

Continue the conversation with the following questions:

- Jesus death is probably the most well-documented event in human history. Do you think his sacrificial love for us was real?
- What should our response to this kind of love be? (Share your own response to put your faith in Jesus.)
- Do you want to respond to Jesus now?

Next Steps

As the conversation comes to a close, keep the door of friendship open by taking some of the following steps:

- End the conversation by asking if you can pray together.
- Set up another meeting a week later to follow up on the dare, to see how it's going, and to continue the conversation about God's love for us. This will allow both of you to have time to process what was discussed.
- Provide a list of scripture verses that help define what love is. Consider keeping this list on your phone so you can easily text it to your friend.

---

[1] NIV

[2] 1 Corinthians 13:4-8a NIV

[3] Robert K. Rapa, "Galatians," in *Romans–Galatians*, vol. 11 of *The Expositor's Bible Commentary Revised Edition*. ed. Tremper Longman III and David E. Garland; Accordance electronic ed. (Grand Rapids: Zondervan, 2008), 630.

I
DARE
YOU

12
...to go to church with me.

I'll never forget Jessie. We met about seven years ago in early March. I was a youth pastor in central Pennsylvania, and Jessie was an average teenage girl. She and her boyfriend showed up for youth group one Wednesday night. They were invited by Derek, who was a regular member of the youth group. Derek invited his friends to church all the time. He wasn't what a lot of youth pastors would consider a "model teenager," having his fair share of problems and challenges, but he was better than most others at inviting his friends to church. He knew church made a difference for him, and he knew it could make a difference for his friends.

Derek introduced me to Jessie and her boyfriend, and, as I did for most visitors, I welcomed them and helped them feel comfortable. After youth group, I said goodbye to Jessie and her boyfriend and Derek, and we cleaned up. The next week they were back, and the week after that. Derek kept inviting them, and they kept on attending. They'd attended three weeks in a row, so when they were missing the next week, I asked Derek about it. He said they'd had something else going on, but Jessie loved coming, so he was sure they'd be back. We didn't know Jessie had already attended her last youth group service.

A few days later, on April 3rd, Derek called me with anguish in his voice. Jessie and her boyfriend had been out for a drive when he'd come around a corner too fast, lost control of the car, and struck a telephone pole. Her boyfriend survived, but Jessie was killed in the accident. Derek was terribly upset, and a few days later we attended the funeral together. We sat in the back because Derek was too emotional to move any closer to the front. Jessie had been his friend, and it would take some time for him to heal from losing her.

In the three Wednesdays Jessie had visited our church, I'd only had a few short conversations with her. We were getting to know her better, but she had mostly stayed quiet and reserved, so I wasn't sure about her faith in Jesus. As friends and family members shared their memories, I sat thinking about what I could have done differently in the time we'd had together. Had I missed an opportunity to talk with her about Jesus? How could I have been more intentional in my conversations with her?

Then, Steve got up to share some memories. Steve was the youth director at the local YMCA, and I was acquainted with him through the local youth pastors' network, but I wasn't aware that he'd known Jessie. Steve shared that Jessie had been active in YMCA programs for several years, and he'd gotten to know her pretty well. Then he said something that shook me, drove me to tears, and caused me to rejoice all at the same time.

"I hadn't seen Jessie for a couple of months, but she showed up at the YMCA about a week ago, and she was different. Jessie had always been a little down and a little depressed, but a week ago she was upbeat and smiling and cheerful. I asked her what was new or different, and she said she'd been going to the youth group at Bethel Assembly of God. She'd decided to follow Jesus, and she said that everything in her life seemed a little different, a little better now."

As Steve finished his remarks, tears rolled down my face. I turned to Derek and I whispered, "Jessie put her faith in Jesus! It's because of you! You invited her to church! You made the difference."

Derek didn't say much at the time, but as the years have passed, he has come to realize the significance of his invitation, his simple challenge to Jessie and her boyfriend to go to church with him. He was unknowingly inviting them to something that would have eternal consequences for Jessie. That's because church is more than just an event or a service; the church is God's primary agent of mission on the earth, a body that worships him, that builds one another up in Christ, and that demonstrates God's love and compassion.

In this chapter, you will be challenged to dare your friends to go to church with you. Belonging to the body of Christ is a critical part of being Gospel-centered, so your friends should already know that church is an important part of your life. With that in mind, don't just dare them to go to church with you once, dare them to go to church with you for a month! Challenge them with this, to see if it will make a difference in their lives. When they ask, "What do you dare me to do?" you reply, "I dare you to go to church with me for one month, and see if it makes a difference in your life."

Gospel-Centered

The church is the body of Christ, and Jesus is the head of the body.[1] It is not something we attend, it is something we belong to. Daring your friends to go to church with you is Gospel-centered, in part because it's impossible to be Gospel-centered without belonging to the body of Christ. When you invite them to church, you invite them to observe the life of the body. When you dare them to go with you for at least a month, you give them a chance to *participate* in the life of the body. This could make a huge difference in the lives of your friends.

Jesus told his disciples in Matthew 18:20, "For where two or three gather in my name, there I am with them."[2] Each time the church gathers together in the name of Jesus, He is present; at youth group, on Sunday mornings, during small group meetings, at retreats and activities. Daring your friends to go to church with you means more than simply asking them to attend an event, it's inviting them to encounter Jesus in the presence of His followers.

Spirit-Empowered

The Holy Spirit is also present when the church gathers in the name of Jesus, often speaking to and through believers. The Apostle Paul explained how this works in 1 Corinthians 12-14, teaching about the spiritual gifts and the way in which they are to be used in the church; which is for the common good of the body.[3] Whenever the church gathers together, if it remains open and sensitive to the Holy Spirit, an experience with the Holy Spirit is sure to follow. When you dare your friends to go to church with you for one month, you will be daring them to experience the power of the Holy Spirit in the midst of the body of Christ.

Personally Responsible for the Mission of God

When Derek invited Jessie and her boyfriend to go to church with him, he had no idea the eternal consequences would be realized so soon. In challenging them to come to church, Derek was taking personal responsibility for the mission of God. However, daring your friends to go to church isn't just about getting them into a position to hear the Gospel, it's also about moving them into discipleship. Part of our personal responsibility is to make disciples, and the church is most often the place where discipleship occurs; it is part of the purpose of the church.[4] When you invite your friends to go with you for one month, you will be inviting them into a disciple-making environment. When they place their faith in Jesus, they'll already feel comfortable as part of the body of Christ.

Have Some Fun

It's always good to have some fun before you move on to the serious dare. Since the serious dare is focused on inviting your friends to church, it might be fun to dare your friends to do something that happens in a normal church service. One of the common things that happens in a lot of churches is "greeting your neighbor," which is a few moments during the service for congregants to say hello to one another.

When your friends ask you to dare them to do something, challenge them by saying, "I dare you to greet and shake hands with at least 10 people." Make sure to be respectful of your surroundings. If it's not an appropriate dare for the time, suggest something else. Whatever happens, have fun and laugh together.

I Dare You

However your friends respond to the fun dare, make sure you thank them and treat them with grace. Transition the conversation by saying, "That's actually not the real dare. What I really dare you to do is to go to church with me. I dare you to go to church with me for one month, and see if it makes a difference in your life." Wait for their response, and then be prepared to answer their questions.

The first thing your friends may ask is, "Why?" This is a natural question, so don't be surprised. Keep in mind that many people have different ideas about church; some good, some bad, and many misguided. Be prepared to share what belonging to the body of Christ means to you, and how going to church has been a positive and enriching experience for you.

You should be able to answer questions about when church is, what time they should be there, and how to get there. Invite your friends to the services or activities that will be most effective for them: youth group, Sunday morning service, small group meetings, activities, retreats. Make sure they feel comfortable; offer to pick them up and bring them with you, and introduce them to your friends.

You should also be ready to have a more lengthy conversation about church. They may need to talk about church, depending on their past experience or concept of it. Here are some questions to start a conversation:

- What do you think about church? What have you heard?
- What has your experience with church been like?
- The Bible describes the church as the "body of Christ." What do you think that means?
- What would make you want to come to church more?

Next Steps

Whether or not your friends decide to join you at church, thank them for allowing you to dare them. If they agree to go to church with you:

- Make sure they know where, when, and how to find you.
- Offer to give them a ride to and from church.
- Invite them to hang out afterwards, and invite some other friends from church to come along.
- Have a discussion about what happened. What was their favorite part? What was the most compelling? What did they think of the worship? What did they think about the message?
- Keep the invitations rolling so they're comfortable coming back.
- After they've been coming for a few weeks, have more discussions. What difference has going to church made in their lives? What do they love most about it?

If they do not agree to go to church:

- Let them know you appreciate and care for them.
- If they are not open to coming to a service, ask if they'd be more comfortable in a small group setting, or at a church activity.

Check in with them in a few weeks; ask them to reconsider.

---

[1] Eph. 1:22-23
[2] NIV
[3] 1 Cor. 12:7
[4] Eph. 4:11-16

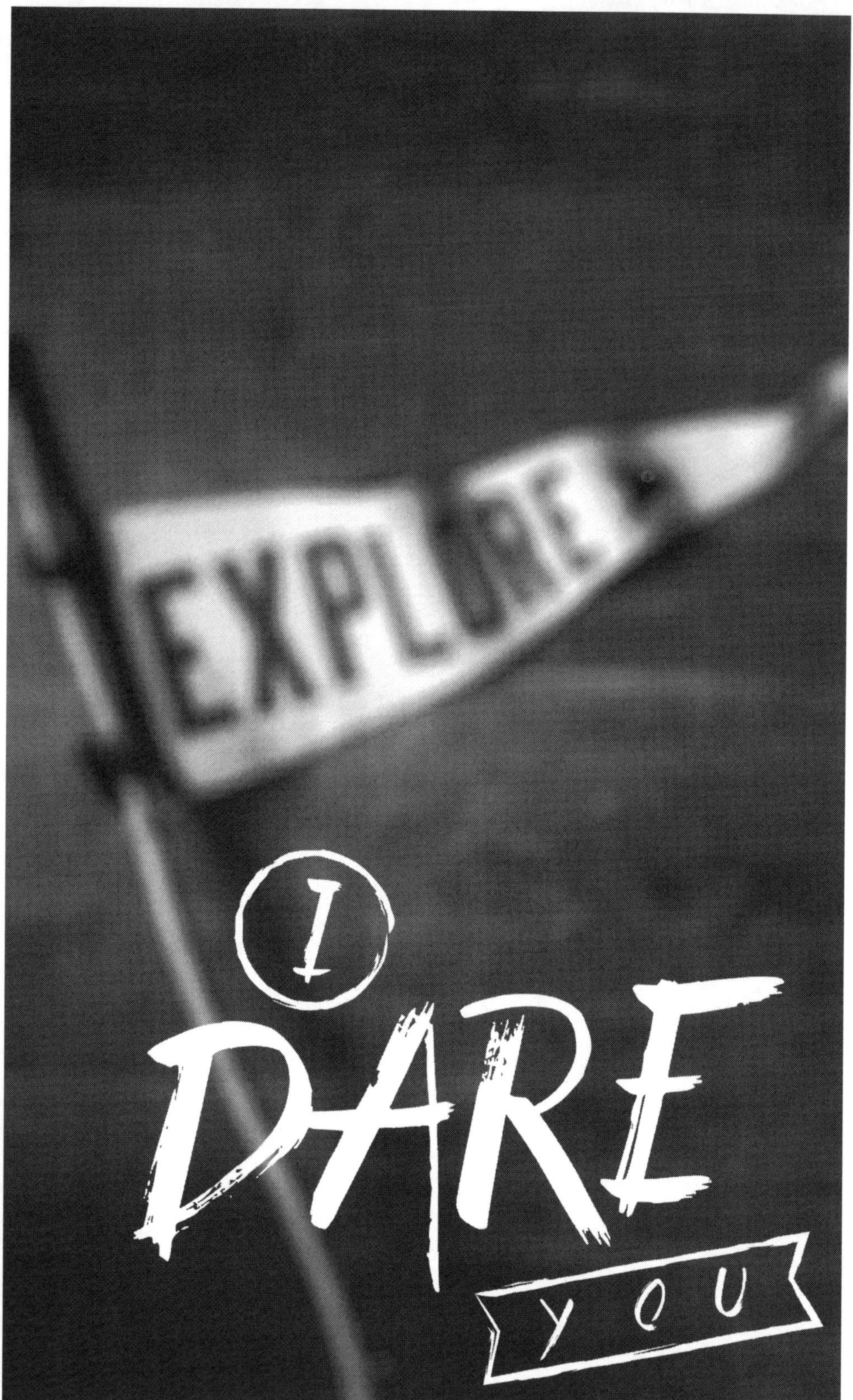
EXPLORE
I
DARE
YOU

13

...to explore your doubts.
Kevin Zurrica

I have a confession to make: I lied. Eight years ago I convinced my four-year-old niece that I was dating Taylor Swift. It all happened so quickly. My niece wanted to share her favorite song with me, and as she belted out some of Taylor Swift's most notable lyrics, I enthusiastically joined.

"Uncle Kevin!" she exclaimed. "How do you know this song?"

"Sweetie, I know this song because Taylor Swift is my girlfriend."

Her eyes widened with awe and excitement. She immediately asked her dad if I was telling the truth, and without skipping a beat, my older brother "confirmed" that I was, indeed, dating Taylor Swift. In one short moment, I became the cool uncle who dates pop-artists.

A few weeks later I received a phone call from my sister-in-law. The story she began to tell me was gold. As my sister-in-law was picking up my niece from Pre-K, she walked into the classroom to see a group of kids conversing loudly in a corner. They were having a competition to see who knew the most about Taylor Swift. My niece pompously walked into the middle of the group, and with a hand on her hip and exaggerated head movements, exclaimed, "Oh yeah?! Well my Uncle Kevin is Taylor Swift's boyfriend!" She turned around and walked off as if to say the competition was over. She walked up to her mother and with a large smile and diva attitude said, "Okay, I'm ready to go."

She continued to believe I had dated Taylor Swift for a few years, and I kept it going as long as I could. I even had a friend's name in my phone changed to Taylor Swift and had her call me from time to time when I was with my niece. However, as she got older she began to doubt my relationship history. More questions were raised, and continually convincing her of this fiction became more difficult. I fear that she has outgrown her belief that I dated Taylor Swift, and quite honestly, I'm surprised it has taken this long for her to realize it…I'm no Casanova.

I have noticed that little children will believe anything you tell them. It's as though they haven't conceived of a world where people could be deceptive or lie. I will admit this level of innocence and naivety has been abused, as I have told many young children fantastic stories and feats that by no means have ever happened. However, as children get older they begin to ask more questions in an attempt to make sense of the world around them. It is a healthy part of cognitive development.

The same can be said of our spiritual development. Each one of us has questions about faith. It is our duty to not run away from questions and doubts, but to explore them and find answers to the questions that we have. In this chapter you will be challenged to dare others to take a very difficult, but necessary journey with you. When asked, "What do you dare me to do?" reply, "I dare you to explore your doubts about faith in Jesus."

Gospel-Centered

Exploring doubts is at the epicenter of the Christian faith. When Jesus was asked what the greatest commandment was, He responded, "…love the Lord your God with all your heart, soul, *mind,* and strength…"[1] Engaging the mind in our quest for faith is so important that Jesus included it in the greatest commandment! Often, doubts and questions stop people from trusting God, but a strong faith in Jesus should only encourage us to explore those doubts.

Nicodemus, a learned Pharisee, was a man with doubts and questions. In John 3, Nicodemus approached Jesus at night and began to ask questions: "How can a man be born again?" and "How can these things be?" He came to Jesus to explore his doubts directly, and in doing so he made great strides towards faith.[2] Church tradition teaches that Nicodemus eventually put his doubts behind him and placed his faith in Jesus. When you challenge friends to explore doubts about faith in Jesus, you'll be taking them on that same journey Nicodemus took.

Spirit-Empowered

Exploring doubts is a difficult challenge. Thankfully, Jesus has sent us a Helper—the Holy Spirit—who teaches us all things.[3] As you begin to explore with your friends the various doubts and concerns they have, be sensitive and listen to the Holy Spirit. Pray that God will work through you to respond in wisdom and grace. Don't be surprised if in exploring doubts the Holy Spirit reveals something new to you or even to your friends.

As your friends begin to explore the doubts they have, the Holy Spirit can speak to them in those moments. With prayer and reliance on God, allow the Holy Spirit to do the difficult work of lifting doubts and convincing them of Jesus. Some doubts are intellectually based, and you might not be informed. That's okay. Be honest. Look up resources together and let the Holy Spirit lead you so that each of you can learn. Don't be afraid of not knowing. The only thing worse than not knowing is not seeking answers. When we explore our doubts, we allow the Holy Spirit to speak to us and convince us of the truth of the Gospel.

Personally Responsible for the Mission of God

Scripture teaches that to be saved, one must not only confess that Jesus is Lord, but also must *believe* that God raised Him from the dead.[4] Belief is easy for some, but seems nearly impossible for others. Even in the first century, the Apostle Paul encountered skeptical people, and needed to provide evidences for their doubts. As Paul recounted the message of Christ, he gave names of people who had seen Jesus, and referenced occasions where multitudes saw Jesus after His resurrection, adding that many of them were still alive at that time.[5] He seemed to be challenging them to find and ask these witnesses about their encounter; he was directly challenging their doubts. Paul directly addressed the doubts of the Corinthian church about resurrection, and we must also directly address the doubts of our friends.

Exploring doubts with the help of the Holy Spirit removes barriers to faith. Paul considered this to be a normal part of his activities when sharing the Gospel. The Message puts it this way, "We use our powerful God-tools for smashing warped philosophies, tearing down barriers erected against the truth of God, fitting every loose thought and emotion and impulse into the structure of life shaped by Christ."[6] Being personally responsible for the mission of God means that we, also, must challenge the doubts of others, "smashing warped philosophies" and "tearing down barriers" by helping them explore their uncertainties.

Have Some Fun

Exploring doubt is a heavy topic; so try to ease into it with some questions that can lead to a discussion about their concerns. When someone approaches you and asks you to dare them to do something, you can begin a conversation by saying, "I dare you to tell me the biggest lie you've ever told." After the person has shared their biggest lie with you, it's always a good idea to ask follow-up questions to keep the conversation fresh and enlightening. Continue to ask simple questions like, "Did the person you lied to believe you, or question whether or not you were telling the truth?" and "Did they ever find out? If so, how?"

I Dare You

Making the conversation light-hearted and fun can create a smooth transition to the dare that you really want your friend to consider. After having some laughs and/or serious reflections about the lies, you can challenge your friend by saying, "Many people feel that the Bible is full of lies and doubt what it says about faith in Jesus. They question what they have heard about Christianity. I Dare You to explore your doubts about faith in Jesus with me."

The next few moments are vital to the conversation. Your friend might begin to get uneasy or want to push away from the conversation. Seriously considering our doubts is an unsettling task as it can highlight our intellectual shortcomings. Your friend may also be afraid of hurting your feelings. Be encouraging! Let your friend know it's normal to have doubts. Do you have a story about a time you doubted your faith? Share it. Show your friend you want to explore the uncertainties together.

Your friend might be pleasantly surprised. You may find out that this is the first time anyone has asked him to seriously consider his thoughts on Christianity. In these moments, be sure to approach his doubts with grace, seeking to understand. If he has created full lists of doubts, politely ask him to explore them with you one at a time. It is important not to dismiss his initial doubts as trivial or imply he lacks common sense. Value his thoughts as a human being, and walk with him to discover answers. Here are a few questions to help explore various doubts:

- What makes this difficult to believe?
- Why do you think it makes you feel that way?
- What would convince you otherwise?
- What factors led to that conclusion?
- What other explanations have you considered?

Your friend might be very excited to tell you every way he finds faith in Jesus absurd! Don't let this intimidate you. Remember, the Holy

Spirit is working within you to speak with wisdom. If you hear accusations, pray for patience and ask the Holy Spirit to help you. Listen for the heart of what your friend is saying. The Holy Spirit may be addressing a root issue or cause for his thinking. Whatever the response, always answer with love and compassion. Affirm your friend on the road to discovery and grow in knowledge together.

Next Steps

Make sure you continue this conversation over the next few weeks, or even months! Here are some suggestions to help guide continued explorations of doubts about Jesus:

- Set up a time to have lunch together to talk, again. Try to identify and discuss other doubts you haven't addressed yet.
- Be honest in your response. If you don't know an answer, tell him you don't know and that you both can look into it.
- Research Christian apologetics. Some authors would include:
  o Norman Geisler
  o William Lane Craig
  o Ravi Zacharias
  o Lee Strobel
  o Greg Koukl
  o Alister McGrath
- If you are having difficulty overcoming your friend's doubts, pray for God to supernaturally intervene. An experience with the Holy Spirit could be what your friend needs to embrace a life of faith.
- Ask your friend to join you to visit a pastor to discuss these doubts.

---

[1] Mark 12:29-30 NASB
[2] See John 7:50-51, 19:39-42
[3] John 14:26
[4] Romans 10:9
[5] 1 Corinthians 15:3-8
[6] 2 Corinthians 10:5 The Message

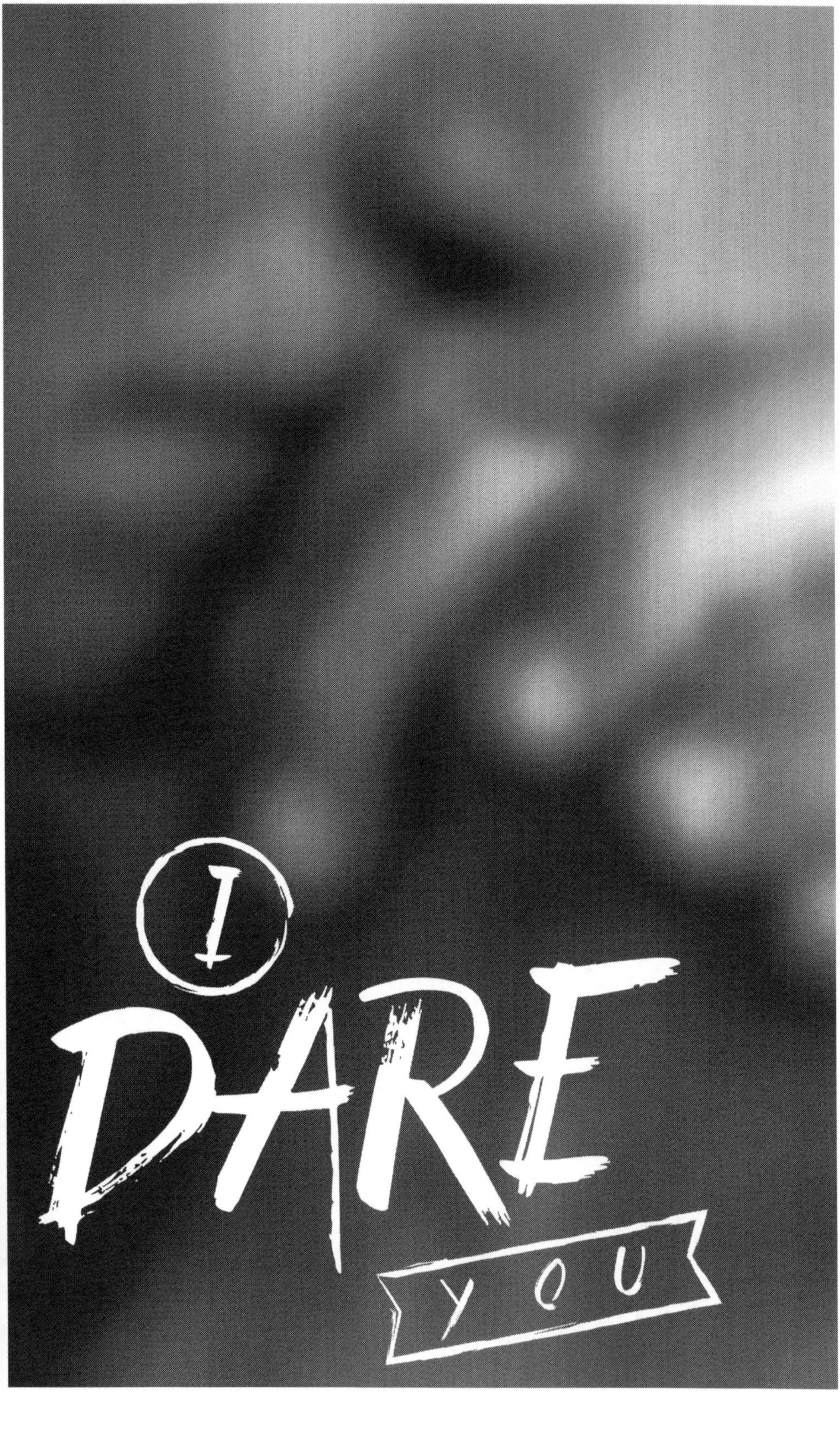
I
DARE
YOU

14
...to talk to God and listen for His answer.
Brad Keller

I have the hardest time listening. I think it's a "guy thing," or maybe it's just human nature. Most of us love to talk about ourselves, but we're not as good at listening.

I have a friend who is a verbal processor. That means in order to work through a problem or an issue he has to talk it out. It doesn't matter what the issue is, he needs to talk about it very thoroughly in order to get it out of his mind and lay it all out. Sometimes it takes just a couple of minutes, but that doesn't happen too often. Most of the time he will talk for more than 30 minutes to process what is happening.

Now maybe you aren't a verbal processor. In order for you to get your problems or issues out, perhaps you need to write them down, or maybe you just need to think things through. I have another friend who is a note-writer and a list-maker. Post-it notes are his best friend. (Honestly he should buy stock in the company.) Whenever he is sitting he is writing something. Maybe it's a to-do list; maybe it's writing down all the accomplishments of the day; or maybe it's just writing down thoughts in a journal. He has lists on his refrigerator, his mirror is covered with post-it notes, and his journal is full of thoughts.

However you process through the challenges of life, whether talking them out or writing them down, the important thing is to communicate—and work through them. That's how it is when we communicate with God. There isn't a right or a wrong way of telling him about our life, our issues, or our problems; but we do have to communicate. God can hear us if we write our struggle out or if we talk it through. God wants to hear about our lives; He wants to hear about our issues, and He wants to hear about our problems. No matter how we process things, He wants us to communicate with Him. Additionally, He doesn't only want us to talk; He also wants us to listen. That is true communication. So then…how do we listen? How does God speak? How does he talk to us?

Jill was in the hospital in an emergency situation. She had a brain hemorrhage and was close to losing her life. The doctors worked feverishly, and many people were praying. Eventually, she came though the dire situation, but there were still many complications from the hemorrhage. She faced new and difficult challenges in her body. She felt alone, frustrated, and sensed that nobody understood her situation.

She began to communicate her feelings to God. She was mad at Him for this situation in her life, and she wanted to hear from Him. She believed the Bible was God's Word and sat down to read it. She didn't know where to start reading, so she prayed—really she shouted—to God. She asked Him to give her some guidance, any encouragement to help because she felt so lost. God led her to read the Book of Job, chapter 23. She had never read Job, and after reading it, she knew God was speaking to her through His Word.

God can talk to us in different ways, as well, including using other people to speak to us. I was trying to decide on a college to go to and was asking God to speak to me about which school to attend. I shared with my parents what I was praying about, and God spoke to them about it. They gave me direction on which college to attend, and I knew in my heart the advice was from God. God also talks to us through supernatural experiences. In Genesis 37, Joseph had a dream from God about his future. In 1 Samuel 3, God calls out to Samuel in an audible voice. 1 Corinthians chapters 12 to 14 explain how God can speak to us through gifts of the Holy Spirit, as well as through the church.

Not only does God want to speak to you, he also wants to speak to your friends who have not yet placed their faith in Jesus. In fact, God is probably already speaking to them, but they do not know it so they are not listening for His message. In this chapter you will be challenged to dare others to pray and communicate with God, and also to listen and let Him speak to them. When they ask, "What do you dare me to do?" you reply, "I dare you to talk to God and then listen for His response."

Gospel-Centered

Jesus, who is at the very center of the Gospel, communicated with God on a regular basis. Luke 5:16 says, "But Jesus often withdrew to lonely places and prayed." If Jesus needed to have regular conversations with God, how much more do we need to have them? In those conversations, Jesus shared his deepest feelings and emotions with God. In Matthew 26:38, Jesus told some of his disciples he was going to pray because he was overwhelmed with sadness. He took his sorrow and pain to God the Father. We should also do the same thing, and when we challenge our friends to do this, we are challenging them to do what Jesus did.

When we challenge others to speak to God and to listen for His reply, we are encouraging them to test God's promises. God promised the prophet, Jeremiah, "Call to me and I will answer you and tell you great and unsearchable things you do not know."[1] We also know that God keeps his promises, as 2 Corinthians 1:20 states, "Whatever God has promised gets stamped with the Yes of Jesus."[2] When you dare your friends to pray and listen, you'll be challenging them to a Gospel-centered practice of exercising faith.

Spirit-Empowered

The Holy Spirit plays an important role when we communicate with God, especially when we are too overcome by our circumstances to focus our prayers. Romans 8:26 explains, "In the same way, the Spirit helps us in our weakness. We do not know what we ought to pray for, but the Spirit himself intercedes for us through wordless groans."[3] The Holy Spirit also helps us hear God's response to our prayers. The Holy Spirit teaches us (Luke 12:12), reminds us of what Jesus has said (John 14:26), and gives others the ability to speak God's word to us (1 Corinthians 12:7-10). When you dare your friends to pray and listen to God, you'll be challenging them to engage with the Holy Spirit.

Personally Responsible for the Mission of God

Many people are open to the idea that a higher power exists. In fact, 98% of the world's population believes in some form of a god.[4] However, they will only connect with the One True God if we take personal responsibility to lead them in that direction. Paul told Timothy, "Proclaim the Message with intensity; keep on your watch. Challenge, warn, and urge your people. Don't ever quit. Just keep it simple."[5] Taking personal responsibility for the mission of God is simple and easy when we challenge others to pray to God and listen for his response.

Have Some Fun

Set up the serious dare by having some fun first. A great way to introduce the concept of listening is to tell your friend, "I dare you to a lip reading challenge." Here's how it works—your friend will put on a pair of headphones and blast some music so he can't hear anything else, then you will say a word or a phrase out loud. Your friend must guess what you are saying by reading your lips. You will get a good laugh out of this one. Take turns so you each get to experience the fun dare. If you don't have any headphones or music with you, you can still play by simply mouthing the words only and not saying them audibly.

I Dare You

After you've had some fun, transition to the real dare. Say, "Actually, what I really dare you to do is talk to God and then listen for His response." This also has the potential to be a lot of fun, mostly because your friend may look at you like you're crazy, but stick with it. It may seem abnormal to your friend, but it's normal to you. Your friend may ask, "Why?" or, "What do I say to God?" Help your friend understand that he can talk to God like a friend, and he can think, say, or write his prayers down. Encourage your friend by suggesting he begin with some of the simple things anyone can talk to God about: the events of the day and how they felt; problems and challenges; good things that are happening; and even hopes and dreams.

Talking is the easy part of praying. Most people have no problem filling a prayer with their feelings, needs, wants, and requests. The more difficult part of prayer is listening, but it's also the most important part. Your friend may have never been challenged to listen to God. He may ask, "What will God say back to me?" Of course, God can say almost anything back to your friend, but encourage him to ask God to speak to directly about one of the following:

- Personal relationships—family and friends
- Emotions—especially the more challenging emotions
- Life issues—job, school, pressures
- Dreams and hopes—What does God think about them?

It would be natural for your friend to ask, "What does God sound like?" or, "How will God answer me?" or, "What should I be listening for?" Help your friend be ready to listen when God speaks to him. Help your friend understand some of the different ways God speaks to us: through the Bible; through others (parents, family, friends, pastors);

through the church; or supernaturally through dreams or spiritual gifts. If your friend is asking God about things that are already spelled out in the Bible, encourage him to consider that God has already spoken to all of us through the Scriptures, and ask him to consider if God is speaking to him through the Word. Be prepared to pray with your friend and encourage him to keep on praying until he hears from God.

Next Steps

Follow up with your friend over the next few days. Ask him:

- What was it like when God spoke to you?
- What did God say?
- What are you doing to apply that to your life right now?
- What does it say about God, that He would speak to you?
- What does that mean to you?

Of course, your friend may not believe or feel like God spoke to him at all. This is normal, especially if he is not used to prayer or listening to God. If that's the case, do not be discouraged, and do *not* discourage your friend. You must encourage him to keep on trying, to open himself up to hearing God's voice through His Word or any other way in which God would speak. Invite your friend to join you for church services over the next several weeks, explaining how God speaks to us through the Body of Christ during the time we spend worshiping and learning together. Challenge your friend with faith—to put aside any doubt that God could speak, and to expect and anticipate God's reply instead. Challenge your friend to pray to God every day for two weeks, eagerly anticipating an answer. If he is looking for an answer from God than can easily be found in Scripture, share those verses with him.

Ultimately, when you challenge a friend to pray and listen, you are leaving the difficult work up to the Holy Spirit. Trust God to answer your friend in the right way and at the right time. If weeks go by, and he still hasn't heard from God, gently encourage him to keep on praying, believing that God will answer in due time.

---

[1] Jeremiah 33:3 NIV
[2] The Message
[3] NIV
[4] http://www.religioustolerance.org/worldrel.htm.
[5] 2 Timothy 4:2 The Message

I DARE YOU

15
...to go to camp with me.
Forrest Rowell

I love camp! I love retreats, conventions, and conferences—they have played a major role in shaping who I am in Christ today. Twenty-seven years ago I attended my first camp; I was ten years old and God changed my life. I wasn't expecting it to happen—it took me completely by surprise! You see, I grew up in a religious home, and I experienced A LOT of church—many churches—over and over again. Every time the church doors opened we were there, but as a 10-year old, I just wanted to stay home and eat a big bowl of cereal while watching cartoons. I was burned out on church...and I was just a kid!

However, I did enjoy participating in Royal Rangers, our church's version of Boy Scouts. One evening after we finished playing a vicious game of "Steal the Bacon," our Commander pulled us all together. He introduced us to a new phrase we had never heard before: "Pow-Wow." He explained that it was a camping experience for us, complete with shooting arrows, throwing hatchets, cooking over an open fire, sleeping in tents, wrestling with friends, and—best of all—no showers for an entire week. That's every 10-year-old boy's dream come true! I packed my bag, got in the van, and travelled six hours to Camp Cedaredge.

Everything our Commander had promised was delivered. However, he had failed to mention one little detail; every night there was a mandatory church service. I was more than disappointed. Like I said, I was burned out on church and simply wanted to have fun. Here I was, having the time of my life, and they burst my bubble by making me go to church.

The service was about what you might expect; a band played some music, a preacher preached, and an altar call was given. I sat there sad and deflated, still disappointed with being pulled away from the "fun" activities. I got even more frustrated at the end of the service, because all the other boys stood in response to the altar call. My friend Craig and I were the only ones left sitting in our seats. We looked at each other and started to make fun of everyone else, but after a few minutes, we both became curious about what was happening at the altar. Soon I stood, along with Craig, and we walked to the altar to investigate.

I'll never forget that night, not because of the preaching or the band, but because that was the night I met Jesus Christ for the very first time in my life! I remember the Creator communicating with me in a very personal way that I had never experienced before. This wasn't just another religious activity—it was a living, breathing experience with Jesus! He let me know that I was loved and that He had a plan and a purpose for my life. God answered many questions for me that night, and since that evening nothing has been the same!

I returned to Camp Cedaredge when I was 16, not for a Pow-Wow this time, but for Youth Camp. A teen-aged young man goes to Youth Camp for many reasons: time away from home, great experiences with friends, wild games, late nights, potential conversations with young ladies, and—of course—powerful experiences with God. Most students leave camp understanding what it is to have a deeper relationship with Jesus, and I was no different. Once again, I responded to an altar call at the end of one of the evening services. I remember running to the front, finding a place to lay on my face and seek God for his will and direction for my life. That night God told me to pursue student ministry as a full-time vocation for my life. It was another amazing experience! I kept that calling to myself; I was so shaken with fear, and humbled in my heart that God wanted to use me, I didn't want to tell anyone.

When I got back home, Mom naturally asked, "What happened at camp?"

That was an easy question to answer because a lot had happened at camp. I told her about the games we'd played, the food we'd eaten, some of the pranks we'd pulled, along with some other funny stories.

Then my mom looked at me and asked a more pointed question, "What did God do in your life at camp?"

Things got real as I described my moment with God. After I'd painted the picture as best I could, she got a big cheesy smile, grabbed the keys to the car, and asked me to take a ride with her. She drove me straight to the church to see my youth pastor and said, "Tell him what you just told me!" From that day forward I was accountable for the call of God on my life...a call I received at camp. I love camp. The experiences I've had there have changed my life.

Now I am a Youth Alive® Missionary and I still participate in camps, conventions, and conferences. I find it so fulfilling because I get to see God pour out His Spirit upon students over and over again. Something special happens when teenagers get away from their day-to-day environment and spend a few days having fun and experiencing God without distractions.

If you've been to youth camp, a youth retreat, or a youth convention or conference where the Word of God was preached with power, authority, and anointing, you've probably also been impacted by the experience. Don't keep the experience to yourself! Why not allow some of your friends, or even acquaintances, to experience God in a similar way by inviting them to come with you? In this chapter you will be challenged to invite your friends to go to camp with you. When they say, "What do you dare me to do?" you reply, "I dare you to go to camp with me!"

Gospel-Centered

Exodus 3-4 contains the story of Moses and the burning bush. Moses did something he'd never done before—he got into God's presence. His curiosity drew him to the burning bush, and soon he realized he was having a conversation with the Creator. The burning bush became an altar in the wilderness. My own curiosity led me to an altar at camp, and I also got into God's presence. That could happen to your friends. They could meet God and experience His power like never before. Camp is a Gospel-centered experience, and when you invite your friends to camp you are taking the first step towards inviting them to the altar. They will be forever changed when God reveals Himself to them!

Spirit-Empowered

Not only did Moses get into God's presence, but He also listened to God's voice. God had a conversation with Moses, and Moses paid attention to what God was saying. We must do the same. We must be Spirit-led and Spirit-empowered. Moses had a few realizations from that conversation:

1. God *is* God. Moses covered his face, humbly afraid when God said, "I AM the God of your father—the God of Abraham, the God of Isaac, and the God of Jacob."[1] Perhaps for the first

time, Moses was awakened to God's existence and His power. God can awaken your friends in the same way.

2. God *sees* us, *hears* us, *speaks* to us, and rescues us. In Exodus 3:7-8, God said, "I have certainly seen the oppression of my people in Egypt. I have heard their cries...I am aware of their suffering. So I have come down to rescue them..."[2] God is still doing the same things today—he sees us, hears us, speaks to us, and rescues us. God spoke through Moses to deliver this message, and he can speak through you to deliver the same message to your friends.

Our Spirit-empowered obedience can lead our friends into their own Spirit-empowered experiences.

Personally Responsible for the Mission of God

The story of Moses continues in Exodus 4:20 "So Moses took his wife and sons, put them on a donkey, and headed back to the land of Egypt. In his hand he carried the staff of God."[3] Moses chose to obey God; he took action to do the things God had asked him to do. He took personal responsibility for God's mission. We must do the same. God wants to use you to invite your friends to youth camp, youth convention, or a youth retreat. Take responsibility, personally, to step out in faith and dare your friends to join you at camp!

Have Some Fun

I believe in having a blast in life! If you are reading this book, chances are you don't mind getting a little crazy either. Before you get to the serious dare, have some fun when your friends ask you the question, "What do you dare me to do?" Ask them to name their favorite movie and pick a scene from that same movie. Dare them to play charades with a random stranger, challenging the stranger to guess the movie they are acting out without using words. Have a good time with it, and consider joining in yourself.

I Dare You

The fun dare should only be the beginning. The real goal is to invite your friends to come to camp with you. When the fun dare has passed, say, "Actually that was just for fun. What I really dare you to do is come to camp with me." Naturally, your friends will want to know why they should go with you. Give them several good reasons! To prepare for this, pick two or three of your favorite memories from camp, convention, or a retreat that impacted your life significantly and share those amazing moments. Spend a few minutes now, thinking through your experiences, and craft a few stories by answering the following questions:

- What attracted you to camp the first time you went?
- What are some of the funniest moments you've experienced at camp?
- Who are you excited to see at camp this year? What makes you excited to see them?
- What are some of the wild and crazy activities you've experienced at camp?
- How has camp given you an opportunity to focus on God?
- What is the most important thing camp has done for your relationship with Jesus?

Trust and believe that God will help you communicate what's necessary to help those friends make the decision to join you at camp. Be bold! Be excited! Be real!

Next Steps

Sometimes your friends will hear your dare and respond with a big "YES!" However, chances are they will need a little more convincing, and a little more time to decide. Take the following steps to continue the invitation over the next few days and weeks:

- Encourage. Continue to pursue your friends and dare them to join you by encouraging them to give it a try. Tell more stories, share more experiences. Don't give up!
- Inform. It's important they receive all the information needed well in advance (dates, times, location, costs, etc.). Parents need these details. A well-informed friend is more likely to come.
- Sacrifice. Offer to pay part of a friend's way to camp. Help with the cost if that's what is holding them back.
- Pray. Pray that God works in your friends' hearts and they would say "YES" to your invitation.

---

1 Exodus 3:6 NLT
2 Exodus 3:7-8 NLT
3 Exodus 4:20 NLT

I

DARE

YOU

Part Three
Conclusion

16
...to put your faith in Jesus.
John Ginnan

"I find your lack of faith disturbing."[1] You might recall the sinister Darth Vader making this infamous disapproving comment. Now you can make it a meme by inserting your own pet peeves: "I find your lack of...*good grammar,* or *factual statements,* or *time away from social media*...disturbing." You get the idea. What brought the infamous black clad villain to make this statement was a taunt he received from a high ranking officer, who boldly and openly questioned Vader's devotion to an "ancient religion," claiming that his faith hadn't helped him at all. Sound familiar? Sometimes people view Christianity as a silly superstition, an ancient religion, with God as some cosmic authority who exists to squash our fun. However, even when people lack faith in the existence of God, we can be confident in persuading them of the reality of God, because even long-held opinions can change—and I've personally seen it happen.

In college I participated in a three-month study program that required me to move to a new place, with new housemates and a new roommate. My roommate and I spent late afternoons and evenings talking about life, history (he could talk about it for hours), and we often talked about faith and God's existence. Through these conversations I started realizing that I was one of the few Christians my roommate knew personally. In sharing my own faith story with him I learned that he considered himself an atheist.

Although my roommate was an atheist, I continued to discuss faith with him because I wanted to help him discover Jesus. Eventually he took me up on an invitation, a *dare,* to attend a church discussion on faith. The title of the discussion was *Christianity: A Psychological Crutch?* His attendance at that church event led him to join a series of church-hosted dinner and discussion nights where nonbelievers, and anyone questioning Christian faith, could explore the claims of Christianity.

After one of the last meetings, my roommate, the group leader and a few others headed to the subway station to catch the various trains that would take them home. While they waited, the group leader challenged my roommate to take Christ at His word—to truly reach out to Jesus. It was *a dare!* My roommate described the next few moments as "being caught in infinity." As the train the others had boarded began to pull away, he was left with an unmistakable feeling that God was real, and this was his opportunity to know God personally. Soon his own train arrived and he boarded to head back to our apartment.

I returned to the apartment later that day. As I approached our room the door was slightly ajar—just enough for me to get a glimpse of my roommate kneeling by his bed. His hands were folded and he was completely still, but his eyes were open. I moved carefully and quietly away so I would not interrupt this stunning and unexpected moment!

I headed to the living room, our daily conversation spot, hoping he'd come out to talk about his day. Not long after, he emerged from the bedroom and joined me, immediately launching into the story. I listened with anticipation, and as the story came to a close he confessed a newfound belief in God's existence! I don't know exactly what he'd prayed that day, but eventually, he placed his full faith in Jesus Christ. I was amazed! My roommate's opinion about God had changed dramatically…and it had all started with a dare!

The ultimate dare, the goal of this entire book, is to dare others to place their faith in Jesus. Every other dare in this book has been about opening the door to faith in Christ, but the purpose of opening the door is to help others walk through it. If you've been daring your friends to pray, or read the Bible, or serve, or go to church with you, but you're still not sure if they have turned their lives over to Christ, then it's time to give the ultimate dare. All of the other dares have been building to this moment, gradually moving them closer to full faith in Jesus, and now it is time to challenge them to make a decision for Christ.

Since you've opened the door to faith though the other dares, when you sense the Holy Spirit directing you, challenge your friends with the ultimate dare. When they say, "What do you dare me to do?" you reply, "I dare you to put your faith in Jesus."

Gospel-Centered

Jesus said, "I am the way and the truth and the life. No one comes to the Father except through me."[2] A Gospel-centered life begins by accepting a Gospel-centered dare—to place one's faith in Jesus as the way to salvation, the embodiment of the truth of God's existence,[3] and the source of life that flows from and is shared with "the very life of God."[4] Truly placing faith in Jesus means that He becomes our way of living, our source of ultimate truth, and the origin of our life's purpose and fulfillment. That's why Paul wrote, "He (Jesus) died for all, that those of us who live should no longer live for themselves but for him who died for them and was raised again."[5]

Daring friends to place their faith in Jesus means challenging them to follow Jesus, which is impossible if not for the Gospel. This is why the Gospel is called the good news: because Jesus makes it possible to live a life we couldn't otherwise live. We can't earn this by our actions—it is a gift of God—it's grace given to us, and it is given to us on the basis of our faith in Him. He lived the perfect life we are not able to live and died the sinner's death we deserved. In beating sin and death through the resurrection, He offers us a new life with Him, one we were always meant to have, to be lived fully for Him.

Spirit-Empowered

One of my favorite quotes comes from Laurence Singlehurst: "The goal of evangelism is to leave people positive for their next Holy Spirit encounter."[6] I love how he paints the picture of how we should expect the Spirit to work. We've already read how the Spirit draws people to Jesus, convicts them of their sin and of God's righteousness. The Holy Spirit is doing the hard work, so we can relax and focus on letting the Spirit speak through us as we dare our friends to put their faith in Jesus.

Not only is the Spirit drawing everyone to Christ, but the Spirit also begins a new work in every person who places his or her faith in God. Titus 3:5-6 tells us, "He (God) saved us through the washing of rebirth and renewal by the Holy Spirit, whom he poured out on us generously through Jesus Christ our Savior."[7] That's exactly what happened in my roommate's life that momentous day—a Holy Spirit empowered washing of rebirth and renewal! When you dare your friends to put their faith in Jesus, you are daring them to have an encounter with the Holy Spirit.

Personally Responsible for the Mission of God

There's nothing much better than a personal touch: warm cookies on a cold day, kind words of introduction when a friend connects you with someone new, knowing that you are welcome when you enter a person's home. Yes, a personal touch makes a huge difference. Personally daring our friends to put their faith in Jesus is the ultimate personal touch. It's more personal than a social media post, and more personal than inviting them to an event. Yes, it can be intimidating, but we are personally responsible to invite our friends to faith in Jesus. And if they truly are our friends, that responsibility becomes a privilege. When you take on this personal responsibility, you communicate how very important your friends are to you, and how important your belief in Jesus is for them.

Have Some Fun

Back in my middle school days I was crazy about free drink refills, which I first discovered at a particular fast food joint. The whole concept grabbed me so deeply, I had this great idea to try to fool the cashier into giving me free refills...on my hamburger. At first I dared a friend to do it, but instead I just took him along as my witness. I am sure I just wanted the audience anyway.

So we approached the cashier and I asked, "Hello, is it 'free refills'?"

"Yes!" she replied.

"Oh, cool," I said as I presented my empty burger wrapper.

Stunned silence followed, and we got a small giggle from the cashier. I thought it was funny at the time, but maybe I was filled with too much sugar and adrenaline. We didn't get "free hamburger refills," but we did get a laugh, and it took some guts to attempt it.

As you wear the *I Dare You* shirt, a fun dare you could use to break the ice with your friends is to dare them to ask for something for free. When they ask, "What do you dare me to do?" you could say, "I dare you to ask a stranger for a pen." Or choose something else: a shoe, a comb, a car...ask for anything! Have fun, but be careful not to take it too far and offend those you and your friends interact with.

I Dare You

However the fun dare turns out, you can transition to the real dare by saying something like "Actually, what I really dare you to do is put your faith in Jesus." Don't feel like you have to keep talking at this point; instead give them time to answer. Even if it creates an awkward silence, your friends deserve time to give a straight and sincere response. They may ask why, or how, so be prepared to answer. There are a lot of great tools or ideas that can help you explain the basics of the Gospel. Here are two of our favorites:

Idea #1 - *Life in Six Words – G.O.S.P.E.L.*[8]

From the word, Gospel, this simple acrostic is helpful to remember the key points of the Gospel in just six words: God, Our, Sins, Paying, Everyone, Life. Six words that make-up the core essentials of the gospel message:

God created us to be with Him.
"Know that the Lord is God. It is he who made us, and we are his" Psalm 100:3a NIV

- God created Adam and Eve in perfect fellowship with Him and with the environment.
- They walked hand in hand with God.

Our sins separate us from God.
"For all have sinned and fall short of the glory of God." Romans 3:23 NIV

- Adam and Eve sinned and became corrupted, depraved and selfish.
- Their sin corrupted all of humanity.

Sins cannot be removed by good deeds.
"All of us have become like one who is unclean, and all our righteous acts are like filthy rags." Isaiah 64:5a NIV

- People have been trying ever since to seek God's favor through righteous good deeds.
- All of our righteous acts are like filthy rags to our perfect, holy God.

Paying the price for sin, Jesus died and rose again.
"But God demonstrates his own love for us in this: While we were still sinners, Christ died for us." Romans 5:8 NIV

- Jesus died on the cross for all our sins, taking our place for the penalty of our sins.
- There is not a sin that wasn't nailed on the cross.

Everyone who trusts in Him alone has eternal life.
"For God so loved the world that he gave his one and only son, that whoever believes in him shall not perish but have eternal life." John 3:16 NIV

- It's faith alone in Christ alone.
- He who believes has everlasting life.

Life with Jesus starts now and lasts forever.
"Now this is eternal life: that they may know you, the only true God and Jesus Christ, whom you have sent." John 17:3 NIV

- It's not just the quantity of life, it's also the quality of life.
- It's eternal, but it is also a personal relationship with God as our Father.

Idea #2 - The Bridge[9]

The Bridge is another simple way to illustrate the gospel message. On a napkin or piece of paper, one could draw and share the gospel message below:

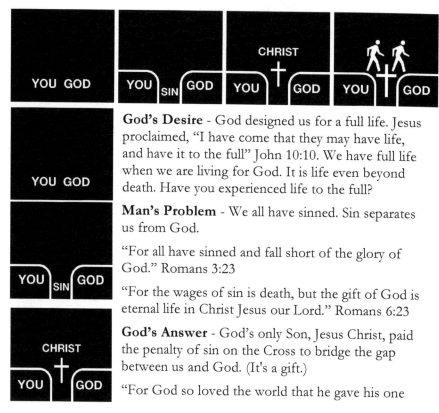

God's Desire - God designed us for a full life. Jesus proclaimed, "I have come that they may have life, and have it to the full" John 10:10. We have full life when we are living for God. It is life even beyond death. Have you experienced life to the full?

Man's Problem - We all have sinned. Sin separates us from God.

"For all have sinned and fall short of the glory of God." Romans 3:23

"For the wages of sin is death, but the gift of God is eternal life in Christ Jesus our Lord." Romans 6:23

God's Answer - God's only Son, Jesus Christ, paid the penalty of sin on the Cross to bridge the gap between us and God. (It's a gift.)

"For God so loved the world that he gave his one

and only Son, that whoever believes in him shall not perish but have eternal life." John 3:16

"But God demonstrates his own love toward us in this: while we were still sinners, Christ died for us." Romans 5:8

"For it is by grace you have been saved, through faith—and this not from yourselves, it is the gift of God—not by works, so that no one can boast." Ephesians 2:8,9

Man's Response - Ask Jesus to forgive your sins, invite Him into your life and follow His direction for living life to the full. "If we confess our sins, he is faithful and just and will forgive us our sins and purify us from all unrighteousness." 1 John 1:9

"That if you confess with your mouth, 'Jesus is Lord,' and believe in your heart that God raised him from the dead, you will be saved. For it is with your heart that you believe and are justified, and it is with your mouth that you confess and are saved." Romans 10:9,10

"Salvation is found in no one else, for there is no other name under heaven given to men by which we must be saved." Acts 4:12

Idea #3 – *Something Amazing*

Something Amazing is a free video to help explain the gospel visually to your friends, available at www.somethingamazing.net.

Praying Together

Now that your friend has had a presentation of the Gospel, the Spirit may be leading him to place his faith and trust in Jesus. Romans 10:9-10 states, "If you declare with your mouth, 'Jesus is Lord,' and believe in your heart that God raised him from the dead, you will be saved. For it is with your heart that you believe and are justified, and it is with your mouth that you profess your faith and are saved."[10] Take this dare to the fullest by asking, "Do you believe Jesus is Lord? Are you willing to say it out loud? Do you believe in your heart that God raised Him from the dead?" Give your friend time to answer each of these questions. Be prepared to have further conversations and discussions.

If your friend expresses faith in Jesus, take the time to pray together. Once someone internally believes and verbally declares Jesus is Lord, that person is saved. The prayer is not what saves; it is faith in Jesus that saves. Praying together helps seal the experience and commitment of your friend, and can be the catalyst for your friend's personal prayer life and conversations with God. Your friend will understand that you both share in being children of God, and that journeying with Christ is something that is designed to happen in community with other believers.

Hesitation and Rejection

If your dare is met with hesitation or rejection, don't take it personally. Instead, ask a few questions to help further the conversation. In this way, you can be a sincere friend who truly cares about what hinders your friends from believing. Here are some questions that can help:

- What keeps you from placing your faith in God?
- If they say they already believe in God, you could ask: What would it look like if you trusted Him every single day?
- Have you ever thought of trusting God with your whole life? What might it look like if you did?

Next Steps

Your friend might take the ultimate dare to place his or her trust in Jesus, but it's also possible that the conversation revealed some obstacles to believing. Here are steps to move forward:

- Thank them for sharing their thoughts about God, and express your gratitude for their friendship. You might remark that sharing their personal thoughts on God and belief is not something people do all the time, and it was meaningful.
- If your conversation revealed some obstacles to belief, let those obstacles direct how you pray for your friend.
- Your church or youth group may have a resource that helps people ask tough questions about Christianity in a relaxed setting. This may be as simple as going out for a burger with your youth leader and your friend. Or it may be inviting him or her to a small group study, or a youth group event.
- When your friends expresses faith and trust in Jesus, make sure to introduce them to a church they can call their own. Emphasize that each church is a local part of the global body of Christ, and they are now part of that global family.
- Your friends can publicly announce their faith in Jesus through water baptism. Encourage this next step in their lives.
- Whether your friends expressed faith in Jesus or not, keep

inviting them to be part of your life and your church. Ease any discomfort they may have by assuring them they are welcome .

- If your friend expressed faith in Jesus, he or she is now also personally responsible for the mission God. Your friend, just like you, is now called to make disciples. The good news your friend received is something to be shared, and you might be surprised how exciting the news of this new personal responsibility can be for a new Christian. Pray together about others you can invite to Jesus.

---

1 *Star Wars: A New Hope*. Written and directed by George Lucas. Produced by Gary Kurtz. Performed by James Earl Jones and David Prowse. USA: Lucasfilm, Ltd., 1977. Film. Darth Vader responds to the admiral's remarks about Vader's devotion to "The Force."

2 John 14:6 NIV

3 Craig S. Keener, *The IVP Bible Background Commentary: New Testament*, Accordance electronic ed. (Downers Grove: InterVarsity Press, 1993), 299.

4 Colin G. Kruse, *John: An Introduction and Commentary*, vol. 4 of Tyndale New Testament Commentaries. IVP/Accordance electronic ed. (Downers Grove: InterVarsity Press, 2003), 294.

5 2 Corinthians 5:15 NIV

4 Laurence Singlehurst. "Address at Forever 2012 Rally," (Harpenden Youth With A Mission, Hertfordshire, United Kingdom, July 26, 2012).

7 NIV.

8 *The GOSPEL* acrostic is copyrighted by Dare 2 Share. Used by permission. See more resources on this idea at www.lifein6words.com

9 *G5 – Growing In The Five Commitments Of A Campus Missionary*, Youth Alive®, 1445 N. Boonville Ave., Springfield, MO, p 141-142.

10 NIV

I
DARE
YOU

17
Daring to be Different

"Thou shalt pass in thy papers, Lee."

Several members of the class chuckled as I looked up from my reading. It was my geometry teacher, and she was waiting for me to pass my test forward along with the rest of my row. I had finished early, and was reading my Bible while I waited for everyone else to finish. I'd been carrying my Bible around school for a couple of weeks, reading it in every bit of free time I could find. Apparently my geometry teacher had noticed, and this was her way of commenting on it. I'd come to expect my classmates to comment on my newfound zeal for the Lord, but this was the first time a teacher had said anything about it.

Even in those days (more than 20 years ago), it was unusual for a student to carry a Bible around, or to be overly "religious" in any way. Students carried all kinds of things around school; many had walkmans or discmans (these were the ancient predecessors to smart phones and music streaming services), food, baseball trading cards, and, of course, school books, papers, pens, and pencils. Students who loved reading often carried a fiction book for study hall, other students carried around tobacco products hidden from sight, and I even remember some of the girls carrying blankets around in case they got cold. We carried whatever we wanted for the day, as long as we could get away with it. However, no one carried a Bible. It just wasn't done.

When I began sharing my faith at school, carrying my Bible around, and challenging my classmates with the Gospel, they started treating me differently. There were some students who poked fun at me, or who obnoxiously engaged in language and behavior they believed would make me uncomfortable. That's always to be expected, and I was ready for it. However, my friends also started acting differently towards me. I started getting left out of certain jokes, didn't get invited to certain parties or get-togethers, and it felt like everyone was just a little more careful with their language when I was around. I didn't really mind any of that, because I probably wouldn't have wanted to participate anyway. They changed their behavior towards me, but the biggest transformation was taking place in my own heart and mind. One of those changes was the realization that I was different because of Jesus; different from who I had been before, and different from my friends now. My geometry teacher's words cut me just a bit; she was pointing out my difference, and she was doing it for all the class to see.

Of course, this didn't come anywhere close to what I would consider persecution. Rather, it's a natural consequence of following Christ. Peter realized this soon after becoming Jesus' disciple, and later wrote, "But you are a chosen people, a royal priesthood, a holy nation, God's special possession, that you may declare the praises of him who called you out of darkness into his wonderful light."[1] We belong to God and that distinguishes us from everyone else. We are different, and that's just the way it is. Our difference is for a purpose; to declare the praises of God, because he saved us from our darkness and brought us into his light. Being Gospel-centered, Spirit-empowered, and personally responsible for the mission of God means we will stand out in many ways from those around us who don't believe in Jesus.

One of the challenges of being different is dealing with the hostility the world has for anything unlike itself. For all the talk of tolerance, anti-bullying, and empathy that goes on today, there remains little hesitation to belittle, discredit, or criticize those who follow Jesus and adhere to Biblical values and belief. That's because tolerance is generally only given to differences within the same value system. The further the world moves away from Biblical values and belief, the greater the hostility towards our differences will become. This isn't new, it's been going on for thousands of years. In its mildest forms, it happens when people point out our differences in a belittling way. In its harshest forms, followers of Christ are imprisoned or put to death because of their faith. By following Christ we are daring to be different. Being Gospel-centered, Spirit-empowered, and personally responsible for the mission of God means challenging the world by our very existence.

The earliest Christians recognized this, and instead of working to blend in with the rest of society, they embraced their difference as part of their identification with Christ. The Apostle Paul wrote how his imprisonment at Philippi made the church more daring in sharing its faith:

Now I want you to know, brothers and sisters, that what has happened to me has actually served to advance the gospel. As a result, it has become clear throughout the whole palace guard and to everyone else that I am in chains for Christ. And because of my chains, most of the brothers and sisters have become confident in the Lord and *dare* all the more to proclaim the gospel without fear.[2]

Paul's imprisonment, a result of his difference from the world, motivated the church to *dare* to preach the Gospel even more than before. In their first letter to the church at Thessalonica, Paul, Silas, and Timothy further explained the situation, "We had previously suffered and been treated outrageously in Philippi, as you know, but with the help of our God we *dared* to tell you his gospel in the face of strong opposition."[3]

They *dared* to tell the Gospel. They embraced their difference from the world, writing "we are not trying to please people but God."[4] They weren't concerned with watering down their message to make it more appealing; they knew their difference was part of their message. They wrote, "we never used flattery, nor did we put on a mask…we were not looking for praise from people…"[5]

My geometry teacher's taunt was quite mild, but it still pointed out my difference. No one else carried or read their Bible in school. I dared to do it, and it provoked a response. It wasn't the first time I'd been belittled for my faith, and it surely wasn't the last. When you challenge your friends to open the door to faith, when you dare them to place their faith in Jesus, you'll be inviting a response. They may respond positively, or they may respond with an insult or taunt. Either way, you'll be putting your difference on full display.

I dare you to do it. I dare you to embrace your difference. I dare you to be Gospel-centered. I dare you to be Spirit-empowered. I dare you to be personally responsible for the mission of God. I dare you to spread the Gospel one challenge at a time.

---

[1] 1 Peter 2:9 NIV
[2] 1 Phil. 1:12-14 NIV, emphasis added
[3] 1 Thess. 2:2 NIV, emphasis added
[4] 1 Thess. 2:4b NIV
[5] 1 Thess. 2:5-6a NIV.

About the Authors

Lee Rogers, Lead Author and General Editor

Lee is a husband to Christine and a father to Judah. He serves as a Youth Alive® Missionary in Pennsylvania and Delaware. An 18-year veteran of Youth Ministry, Lee is a graduate of the University of Valley Forge, and a Doctoral student at Regent University. He is the author of *Initiate: Powerful Conversations that Lead to Jesus,* and the lead author of *God So Loved: a student's guide to sharing Jesus at school.*

 @TheLeeRogers

CONTRIBUTING AUTHORS

Jason Forsman is a Youth Alive® Missionary. His mission is to bring hope to students. He loves spending time with his family, friends, and Boston Sports. He has worked with every age of student and loves serving in all aspects of ministry. He lives in Michigan with his wife Lindsay, and their daughter and son. Their motto is "teamwork makes the dream work."

David Freeland is the Youth Alive® Missionary in Maryland, Virginia, West Virginia, and Washington D.C. He received his Masters degree from Liberty University. He and his wife Jillian reside in Virginia with their four daughters.

John Ginnan has served in local church youth ministry for over twenty years and was once a public school teacher. Currently he leads Youth Alive® in New York with his wife Caity. They enjoy life together with their 3 little kids, their travels together, and friends across the state along with New York's diverse tastes, cities and cultures.

Kent Hulbert currently serves as the National Youth Alive® Missionary, leading Youth Alive® nationally. Kent has been ministering to teenagers for over 3 decades. Kent has two grown children and resides with his wife Staci in Nixa, MO.

Bradly Keller has been working with students for over 20 years. He has worked with Young Life, Fellowship of Christian Athletes and now Youth Alive®. His heart is to see students connect with Christ and share the hope of Christ with their friends.

Jessica Riner is a Youth Alive® Missionary in Georgia. She's a graduate of Southeastern University in Lakeland, FL and has served in student ministries for 17 years. She's passionate about investing in the lives of students and seeing them grow to their full potential in Christ. She and her husband, Ken, reside in Central Georgia. Jessica loves anything with peanut butter, dark chocolate, and almonds.

Forrest Rowell is a graduate of Southwestern Assemblies of God University. He married his high school sweetheart, Hannah, and they have six children. They are Colorado natives and have served 15 years in full-time student ministry. They love Jesus the American teenager! Forrest is a Youth Alive® Missionary in the Rocky Mountains.

Ben Russell has served as Youth Alive® Missionary in Alabama for the past 8 years & has been in student ministries for 16 years. He is a graduate of Southeastern University in Lakeland, Fl. He is married to Terra & has 2 kids - Knox & Anna.

Wes Sheley is a Youth Alive® Missionary in Oregon and Idaho, and a 20-year veteran of youth ministry. He is President and Co-Founder of Impact 24/7, building bridges between communities and local schools through school adoption projects, leadership training, and school assemblies. He is a graduate of Southwestern Assemblies of God University. He is Married to Carrie and has two kids—Nic and Jaelyn.

Kevin Zurrica has been working with students from various socio-economic backgrounds for the last 10 years. His passion is to see students engage with the Gospel and be transformed by its truth. He currently serves as Youth Alive® Director for Southern New England, overseeing ministry to secondary schools in Connecticutt, Massachusetts, and Rhode Island.

Also available from Missional Basics

Of all the challenges a Christian faces today, sharing the Faith with others can be one of the most intimidating. But it doesn't have to be! What if sharing the Gospel could occur naturally in a conversation about family, hobbies, or dreams?

Initiate: Powerful Conversations That Lead To Jesus
Lee Rogers

Anyone can learn to have powerful conversations, great relationships, and discover natural opportunities to share the Gospel in the process!

Available in print and eBook at www.initiateconversations.com, Amazon.com, Barnes & Noble, and iBooks.

Accompanying Sermons and Small Group Lessons also available at www.initiateconversations.com.

Also available from Missional Basics

God so loved the world. God so loved my school. GOD SO LOVED is a student's guide to sharing Jesus in the largest and most accessible mission field in the United States—the public school. Middle and High schools are filled with diverse groups of people, all of whom need to hear about Christ: artists and athletes, academics and craftsmen, the hurting and the average, everyday teenager.

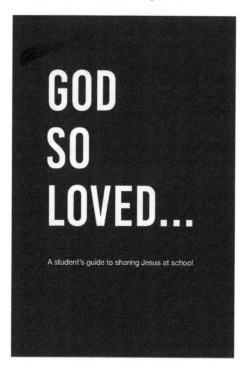

GOD SO LOVED... a student's guide to sharing Jesus at school

GOD SO LOVED is designed to help Christian students share Jesus through serving and conversations with more than 30 distinct groups at school and beyond. This book is filled with real life stories, practical ideas, and powerful questions that lead to great conversations. GOD SO LOVED doesn't begin on a foreign mission field, GOD SO LOVED begins in your school.

Available in print and eBook at www.initiateconversations.com, Amazon.com, Barnes & Noble, and iBooks.

Accompanying Sermons and Small Group Lessons also available at www.initiateconversations.com.